THE

GOVERNMENT BENEFITS HANDBOOK

How to Collect Grants and Benefits from the Government

Fully Updated to include 1994-95 Benefit Rates

by
Bill Habets

Published in Great Britain by Carnell Limited,
37 Salisbury House, London Wall, London EC2M 5PJ.

Copyright © MCMXCIV by Carnell Limited.

Typeset by SJ Design and Publishing, Bromley, Kent.

Printed by Repro City Limited, London.

ISBN 1-85779-370-6

Table of Contents

Page

	Foreword	5
1	How To Collect Social Security Benefits At Any Age	7
2	How To Collect Family Benefits	14
3	How To Collect Income Support And Other Social Security Benefits	30
4	How To Collect Social Fund Loans, Grants And Payments	43
5	How To Collect Sickness Benefits	50
6	How To Collect Invalidity And Disability Benefits	57
7	How To Collect Free Prescriptions And Other Health Benefits	72
8	How To Collect Unemployment Benefit	80
9	How To Get Free Job Training And Interest-Free Careers Loans	88
10	How To Collect Grants And Loans To Start Your Own Business	93
11	How To Collect Housing And Other Associated Benefits	98
12	How To Get Free Legal Assistance	106
13	How To Collect War Pensions And Benefits	113
14	How To Collect Education Grants And Loans	124
15	How To Collect Retirement Pension	130
16	How To Get Well-Paid Government Jobs	138
17	Other Sources Of Help And Advice	142
18	How To Get Valuable Free Information	147
19	How To Collect Benefits Abroad	152

Appendix A — 161
Common Rules For Income Support, Housing Benefit, Council Tax Benefit, Disability Working Allowance And Family Credit

Appendix B — 165
Living Together As Husband And Wife

Appendix C — 167
Extra Benefits For Dependants

Appendix D — 169
How To Appeal

FOREWORD

Bureaucrats Made This Book Necessary

Millions of pounds will be made available to citizens of this country this year through a wide variety of Government programmes and the scale of benefits will range from a few pounds a week to literally tens of thousands of pounds for a single claimant.

Yet, many people are quite unaware of the size of the help available and don't get their fair share of this mammoth redistribution of the national wealth as they continue to miss out on benefits that are rightfully theirs.

The purpose of this book is to redress that balance by giving you, the reader, the information you need to identify what your entitlement is and claim it. Great pains have been taken to ensure that this is the most concise, easiest to read handbook on the subject available anywhere and it is my hope that you will not only find it interesting but rewarding as well, as you spot benefits you're eligible for and entitled to claim.

That you're entitled to one benefit or another – if not now, then some time in the future – is almost a certainty because Government help programmes encompass such a wide range of situations and circumstances that there are few people indeed who haven't got an entitlement of some sort. But, although it's all very well to be entitled, how are you going to claim what is owed to you if you don't know about it in the first place? And, that is where the Government tends to fall down because – with some very rare exceptions – precious little publicity is given by its bureaucracy to the many benefits that it provides.

The situation isn't helped, either, by the frequent changes that take place in benefits. For example, this year will see the introduction of drastic alterations to maternity-linked benefits. It has also been proposed that wide-sweeping changes will take place in both sickness benefit and invalidity benefit next year. This book fills the information void by providing you with full details of all the current schemes and programmes, including the rules for eligibility and how to go about claiming your due, as well as giving you advance notification of the pending changes.

There is, of course, no question that you should claim any benefit to which you're entitled. To do otherwise would be like not wanting to bother your insurance company if your house were to burn down.

When times are good, the Government is quick enough off the mark to collect its share of your earnings, usually taking it off your pay before you even get it. So, as you've paid your enforced premiums, you're entitled to collect when it's your time to do so. Incidentally, even if you've never paid either income tax nor National Insurance contributions, you have still contributed to the Government coffers because that's exactly what you did every time you bought something that carried Value Added Tax and this nowadays even includes the fuel you use to keep your home warm.

A brief word about how this handbook is organised. Each chapter deals with benefits that are linked because they are meant to help a particular group of people. Full details are given in each case about how you can obtain extra information if you need it as well as how you should apply if you're eligible. *All the rates quoted are correct at the time of going to press, but many of them will, of course, be increased next year.* Additionally, it must be pointed out that the legislation which governs benefits is very complex indeed and that the information in this book should not be treated as a complete and authoritative statement of the relevant law.

Finally, I must acknowledge with grateful thanks all those who have helped me by providing the information that fills these pages. They are too many to mention individually, but special thanks are due to Frank Gresty, Sue Cork, John McCaughey, Stephen Will, Henry Elstead, Duncan Haigh and Richard Oliphant.

Bill Habets

1 How To Collect Social Security Benefits At Any Age

"Security for all from the cradle to the grave" – that was the proud boast with which the Welfare State was first introduced. Now, nearly 50 years later, that statement still rings true because there are indeed benefits to cover just about anyone in any age group.

In fact, it could be claimed that the social security system helps you even before you are born – by providing maternity benefits for your mother – and continues to provide protection after the grave – by giving pensions and allowances to your surviving dependants.

Today's social security system is quite different from how it was in the early days – some critics say that successive Governments have diluted the founding principles to such an extent that it bears little resemblance to what preceded it – yet to understand it fully it is worth taking a brief look at its ancestry.

THE EARLY DAYS

It all began with the now famous Beveridge Report of 1942 produced by Sir William Beveridge (later Lord Beveridge) who had been nominated to head a committee set up by the Government, at the suggestion of then powerful trade unions, to review existing National Insurance arrangements.

The major recommendations of that report were incorporated in two Acts of Parliament in 1946, the National Insurance Act and the National Insurance (Industrial Injuries Act). Together these laid down the foundations for today's social security system by:

a) Creating the National Insurance Scheme which became operative in 1948.

b) Providing replacements for previously existing provisions for pensions, unemployment and workmen's compensation.

c) Ensuring that everyone of working age – with the exception of certain non-employed, including married women – would pay national insurance contributions.

d) Setting levels of mandatory contributions and classifications for different groups, such as the employed, self-employed and non-employed.

e) Linking these contributions to specific benefits which depended on the contributions record of the claimant.

As was to be expected, it was found that there were many who were not covered at all or only inadequately by these provisions. It was to cater for these groups that the National Assistance Board was created in 1948 with the task of providing non-contributory help based on an assessment of the needs and means of the claimant.

THE INTRODUCTION OF NEW BENEFITS

It is from these two strands of contributory benefits and means-tested benefits that today's system has evolved. Many minor changes, of course, were made by successive Governments over the decades, but a fundamental reform took place with the Social Security Act 1986, most of which was implemented in 1988. The changes included:

a) The abolition of Supplementary Benefit and the introduction of Income Support to replace it. Still a means-tested benefit – although the phrase was now 'income-related' – Income Support was meant to top up the income of those whose means were judged to be insufficient for their needs.

b) Family Credit was launched to replace the old Family Income Supplement. Also income-related, Family Credit was to provide extra income for working families with children.

c) The Social Fund was created to provide extra non-contributory benefits – although some of these were to be in the form of repayable loans – for people with exceptional expenses.

d) Housing Benefit qualifying income levels were brought in line with those for Income Support and assessment would now be based on net income. This would help avoid the so-called unemployment and poverty traps which often meant that for some people there was little incentive either to seek work or work harder and earn more.

THREE GROUPS OF BENEFITS

With the addition of these new schemes, Social Security benefits can now be clearly defined as belonging to one of three basic groups:

First of all, there are the **contributory benefits**. These, as envisaged by Beveridge so long ago, still are available only to those who have paid or been credited with enough of the right kind of National Insurance contributions. The main contributory benefits include: Unemployment Benefit, Sickness Benefit, various Invalidity Benefits, Maternity Benefits, Widow's Benefits and Retirement Pension.

Then there are the **non-contributory benefits** which are available to everyone who is eligible and qualifies no matter what their National Insurance contributions record may be. Major members of this group include: Guardian's Allowance, Child Benefit, Attendance Allowance, War Pensions and several Allowances for the disabled.

Finally, there are the **income-related benefits**: Income Support, Family Credit, Social Fund and Housing Benefit. You'll get these if your circumstances warrant it and your National Insurance contributions record is not taken into account when determining eligibility.

From the above, it would seem that there is indeed a benefit of some kind for everyone who might need one. And, so there is, but the fact that there is a benefit does not necessarily mean that it pays enough to meet the reasonable needs of claimants and there is a lot of evidence to support that view. For example, many old age pensioners find it necessary to claim Income Support as well; proof, say the critics, that at least for some the state retirement pension and its various supplements remains inadequate in itself.

A FAIR SYSTEM?

A further criticism of the benefits system is that it can be grossly unfair in application. For example, diabetes patients who need drugs for their condition get their prescriptions free while glaucoma sufferers who, unless they are treated by surgery, will also be dependent on drugs for the rest of their lives, have to pay for them. There are many more such inconsistencies and anomalies.

Another major discrepancy lies in the way that the disabled old are treated as compared with their younger counterparts because several benefits are either not available or reduced if the disability occurred after state pension age.

There are many more such examples to be found. However, the aim of this book is not so much to criticise the system but to show you how to make it work for you so that you may claim all you're entitled to. And, '**claim**' is a very important word in this context because it is a mainstay of Department of Social Security policy that benefits must be 'claimed' – no one is going to chase you to make a claim just because you're entitled. One noteworthy exception to the foregoing is the state Retirement Pension when you will usually be contacted by the DSS some months before your reach pensionable age, but even then you have to claim it.

Of course, the idea that benefits must be claimed is quite defensible for several reasons, including the one that it would be quite impossible to track down potential beneficiaries in many instances. What is not quite so defensible is the comparatively poor record that the DSS has had in the past in publicising what is available. In fairness, however, it must be added that this is slowly changing and a substantial advertising campaign was used to promote Family Credit when it was launched. Cynics might say that this was partially because this particular benefit might convince those who were claiming Unemployment Benefit and Income Support that they would actually be better off in work.

Be that as it may, it can be safely said that many benefits are not at all well-known – and, of course, you can't claim what you don't know about! This book, we hope, will enable you to identify your entitlements and claim them.

THE UNCLAIMED MILLIONS

Undoubtedly, there are many millions of pounds of unclaimed benefits of all kinds. But just how large this sum is remains a matter for some conjecture. The DSS itself is only able to provide figures relating to three major benefits: Housing Benefit, Income Support and Family Credit. The most recent set of figures available at this time covered take-up estimates for the year 1989, although a more up-to-date version was due for publication. There is, however, no particular reason to believe that these will show any drastic change in the broad picture.

When considering the figures that are available – and which were prepared by the Government Statistical Service – several points need to be kept firmly in mind:
1) Those in full-time self-employment are excluded from the figures because, says the DSS, of the difficulty in determining accurately whether they are entitled to receive income-related benefits.

2) Also excluded are those people not living in private households and resident in, for example, institutions.

3) The DSS point out that all these estimates are open to a significant margin of error.

4) All claimed and unclaimed amounts have been rounded to the nearest £10 million.

Taking into account these points, here are some key facts regarding the take-up estimates for 1989:

☐ **Housing Benefit.** The total claimed was £4,790 million, whilst £470 million remained unclaimed, adding up to a take-up rate of 91% on the basis of expenditure. However, if instead of looking at the costs, the take-up rate is calculated on the basis of how many of the eligible recipients actually claimed the benefit the situation is somewhat different: 5,060,000 recipients received Housing Benefit and 1,070,000 who were eligible didn't because they didn't claim it. This means that the take-up rate based on 'caseload' – as the jargon has it – was only 83%.

☐ **Income Support.** £6,610 million was claimed and £1,020 unclaimed, adding up to an expenditure-based take-up rate of 87%. The caseload-based take-up rate was, however, only 75% with 4,030,000 recipients and 1,320,000 eligible non-recipients. It's also worth noting that the caseload-based take-up rate for Income Support for eligible pensioners fell to only 67% – or just more than two out of three.

☐ **Family Credit** (in this instance the estimates cover the period from April 1988 to December 1989). The amount claimed was £300 million a year and £160 million remained unclaimed, adding up to an expenditure-based take-up rate of 67%. The caseload-based take-up rate was only 57% with 250,000 recipients and 190,000 eligible non-recipients.

STAGGERING AMOUNT REMAINS UNCLAIMED

In all fairness, it must be pointed out that the take-up rates on certain other benefits are substantially higher and that a few of them like the Retirement Pension and Child Benefit probably have a take-up rate in the high nineties of percentage points. On the other hand, there is every reason to believe that more obscure benefits – such as Guardian's Allowance or Invalid Care Allowance – have an even lower take-up rate.

It's impossible to say exactly how much money is not distributed because it is unclaimed, but one can make certain assumptions based on the foregoing figures and a safe estimate surely must be that at least 10% remains unclaimed. If this is the case, it means that in excess of a staggering £6,000 million or more is waiting to be claimed. That figure relates only to DSS benefits with millions and millions more being available, but unclaimed, for eligible beneficiaries from Housing Renovation Grants and other Government programmes.

Then there are, of course, other sources of Government grants, loans and benefits, all of which no doubt have less than a hundred per cent take-up rate. Even making a modest allowance for these and adding this to the previous figures would mean that perhaps something like £10,000 million or more remain unclaimed by those who would have been entitled to their share if they, first of all, had known about it and, secondly, put in their claim.

From this it can be seen that it will pay you to read this book with care for the chances are high that in it you will discover some benefit to which you're entitled or will become entitled sooner or later.

THE FUTURE

If some of the above seemed to be knocking the DSS, that was not the intention, for the organisation is itself taking major steps to improve its performance. For example, there is a very interesting initiative by the Benefits Agency called *Toward 2000*. The aim of this project is to provide a *One Stop* service in which all the BA benefits business of a customer can be dealt with through one point of contact. One Stop is being introduced in three stages. The first of these stages – *One Place* – is to be implemented by July 1994 and under this scheme customers can obtain advice, claim benefit and report a change of circumstances at their local office, no matter where the benefit case is handled. So far no dates have been set for the implementation of the next two stages of One Stop, which are *One Person* and *One Time*. One Person will mean that customer enquiries should be dealt with through one person at any outlet; One Time should mean that most business will be completed through one contact point there and then.

The DSS has also massively extended its *Freeline* service which you can call on 0800 666 555 to get general information and advice.

Currently this helpline deals with some 50,000 calls a week and is staffed by 230 operators. Freeline also provides:

□ Ethnic lines in four languages: Urdu (0800 289 188); Punjabi (0800 521 360); Chinese (0800 252 451); and Welsh (0800 289 011).

□ A special service for the disabled, the Benefit Enquiry Line (0800 882 200) which can also offer a forms completion service.

However, these improvements, welcome though they are, will only go a small way towards filling the information gap. Much more will need to be done until general awareness of benefits is raised to such an extent that take-up rates begin to near the 100% mark for all benefits. Critics, of course, argue that Government has a vested interest in keeping claims down because if we were all to receive everything that we're entitled to there would have to be massive additional funding. That may be so, but the Government enforces a deal upon its citizens by saying, in effect, "We will take money from you in contributions, income tax and VAT and use these premiums to create a National Insurance system which will pay you benefits under certain circumstances." It is our right to demand these benefits when they become due because, after all, we paid for them in the first place.

2 How To Collect Family Benefits

A very large part of Social Security resources are earmarked to provide what might be described as 'family benefits', that is benefits which directly or indirectly will improve the financial situation of a family as a whole.

Although these various benefits are linked to specific circumstances, their overall effect is that of helping to provide better living circumstances. For example, if we take a look at Child Benefit, which is linked directly to the number of children in a family, it is quite clear that the money received under this scheme does not necessarily only help the child for whom it is provided, but instead becomes part of the total household funds. In this context, it is interesting to note that Child Benefit is one of the largest Government payouts with £5,767 million being distributed each year to nearly seven million families with a total number of children of more than 12 million.

This chapter is devoted to these 'family benefits', some of which are very well-known – like the comparatively new Family Credit scheme – and others more obscure, such as the Guardian's Allowance.

We'll begin by examining ...

FAMILY CREDIT

This is currently being received by some 500,000 families at a total cost of £1,091 million. On average each family gets more than £43 a week. Of course, some of the beneficiaries get a good deal less than the average and many get a great, great deal more. How much you can get depends on the number of dependant children you have, their ages, and your income and savings.

The DSS sum up the scope of this scheme when they describe it as 'extra money for working people with children' on the cover of one of their leaflets. And, that is exactly what it is, because to qualify for it, you have to be in work and you also have to have at least one child.

The three specific questions to which you must be able to say 'yes' to have a chance of qualifying for Family Credit are:
1) Are you – or your partner – working at least 16 hours a week?

2) Do you – or your partner – support at least one child who actually lives with you?

3) Do you – and your partner – have £8,000 or less in savings between you?

If you've been able to say 'yes' to these three questions, you may be able to claim Family Credit.

Obviously, there's more to it than just that and there are various conditions that claimants have to meet as the amount of Family Credit payable is based on four key factors.

1) How many children there are in the family.

2) The age of the children.

3) How much money is coming into the household every week.

4) How much the family has in savings.

Let us now look at each of those conditions in greater detail.

1) Number of Children. Children in this context may also mean children who are not necessarily your own but may be your partner's through a previous marriage and so on. The key factor here will be whether the child is actually living with you.

2) Age of the Children. This matters because there are different rates of 'credit' according to age. More about this later.

3) Your Income. A very important point because what you might get becomes less as your income goes above a certain point. Income in this case broadly means all of the following: take-home pay from employment; business profits (after allowable expenses); some Social Security benefits (but these exclude Child Benefit, One-Parent Benefit, Attendance Allowance, Disability Allowance, Housing Benefit and Council Tax Benefit). Income also means, for example, maintenance payments (but excluding the first £15 of this) or rent paid to you by boarders or sub-tenants.

4) Your Savings. Although you cannot get Family Credit if you've got more than £8,000 in savings, smaller amounts – between £3,000 and £8,000 will affect what you might get. Savings under £3,000 have no effect; see **Appendix A – Common Rules** at the end of this book for a fuller explanation.

Will you be entitled? Check the second page of your Child Benefit order book and there you will find how much weekly income your family can have coming in and still be entitled to the minimum payment of 50p Family Credit each week. If your benefit is paid into a bank or building society account, this information will be included in your award notification.

How much do you get? The amounts are highly variable because the factors taken into consideration also vary so much, but there is a formula by which you can work out your entitlement.

The first thing to do is to work out the maximum Family Credit you might be entitled to. You do this by adding up the following weekly credits: adult credit (for one or two parents, the amount remains the same) £44.30; for each dependant child, aged 18 – £32.20; aged 16-17 – £23.05; aged 11-15 – £18.55; aged under 11 – £11.20. This means, for example, that if you have two children aged 7 and 14, the maximum Family Credit payable would be £74.05, made up as follows: £44.30 of adult credit; £18.55 for the oldest child; and £11.20 for the youngest one.

The next thing to work out is your total income, following the guidelines outlined above.

Then you have to take into account the 'applicable amount' – which is an earnings threshold level – which currently stands at £71.70 weekly. If your income is lower than this, you'll get the maximum Family Credit.

However, if your income is greater than the applicable amount, there is a further calculation you have to do and this consists of, first of all, deducting the applicable amount from your income, then taking 70% (that's known as the prescribed percentage) of the resulting figure from your maximum Family Credit – what's left will be the amount of Family Credit you're entitled to.

Let's see how this works out in practice in the following examples.

Example One:
George and Mildred Johnson have one child aged 10. Their savings are less than £3,000 and George earns only £70 a week because the only job he could find was part-time.
First of all, work out the maximum Family Credit:

$$\text{adult credit} = £44.30$$
$$\text{credit for child under 11} = £11.20$$
$$\text{total credit} = £55.50$$

As the income of £70 is less than the applicable amount, the Johnsons will be entitled to the maximum Family Credit for them which is, of course, £55.50 a week.

Example Two:
The Westons have three children, aged three, eight and eleven. The family's income is £110 and they have no savings.
So to work out the maximum Family Credit:

$$\text{adult credit} = £44.30$$
$$\text{plus two child credits of £11.20 each, total} = £22.40$$

plus one child credit = £18.55
adding up to a maximum Family Credit = £85.25
The family's earnings of £110 exceed the applicable amount of £71.70 by £38.30. Therefore, the family's maximum credit is reduced by 70% of the excess figure of £38.30 which works out at £26.81.
The total Family Credit payable is their maximum credit (£85.25) less £26.81 which leaves £58.44 payable weekly.

Example Three:
The Greens have two children, aged 12 and 14. They have no savings and their net income (excluding Child Benefit) is £80 a week.
Once again, first work out maximum Family Credit:

adult credit = £44.30
plus two child credits of £18.55 each = £37.10
for a total = £81.40

The Greens' income of £80 exceeds the applicable amount of £71.70 by £8.30, so they have to deduct 70% of the £8.30 (or £5.81) from their maximum Family Credit of £81.40 which means that they are entitled to £75.59 a week.

Working out what your Family Credit might be is not that simple a task and the best thing to do if you think you might be entitled is to apply for a Family Credit claim pack (*ref FC1 Wallet*) which you can get from DSS offices, Post Offices or by ringing the DSS Family Credit order line 0800 500 222 anytime (you won't be charged for the call). The claim pack contains more information and a very useful table which covers most family situations and incomes. Although the table stops at weekly incomes of £237 a week that doesn't mean that you can't get Family Credit if you earn more than that – you can if you have enough additional credits for more children than are covered by the table.

You can get more information about how Family Credit might work out in your own circumstances by ringing the *Family Credit helpline on 0253 500 050*. This special helpline is open from 7.30am to 6.30pm, Mondays to Fridays.

QUESTIONS AND ANSWERS ON FAMILY CREDIT

Q: Who makes the claim for Family Credit – is it the husband or the wife?

A: For two-parent families, it must be the woman who claims, but there are exceptions to this, such as in cases of mental instability.

Q: Who actually decides what I will get?

A: Decisions on claims are made by Independent Adjudication Officers. They should, according to the DSS, make a decision 'so far as it is practicable' within 14 days and that decision will be given to you in writing.

Q: What if I have just started work and need money quickly?

A: For those people who have been unemployed and in contact with the Department of Employment, the method of dealing with Family Credit claims referred through the Client Adviser service has been streamlined. For other people, such as lone parents, a similar procedure has been set up involving liaison between local Social Security offices and the Family Credit unit. These procedures are used where it is clear that there is a need to get Family Credit paid quickly when someone has just started work, and the vast majority of these claims are cleared within a week.

Q: When does my entitlement become effective?

A: Entitlement to Family Credit takes effect from the beginning of the next Family Credit week – these run from Tuesday to Monday – after the date you put in your claim.

Q: How is Family Credit paid to me?

A: Once your claim has been approved by the DSS, you will be given a choice as to how you wish to receive payment – either into your bank or building society account, or with a book of orders you can cash at a Post Office. Awards of £4.00 a week or less are paid as a lump sum at the start of the award.

Q: For how long do I get the payment?

A: Family Credit is awarded for 26 weeks at a time. Should your earnings go up during that period, the payments will still remain unchanged. The DSS will send you a new claim form six weeks before the expiry of your current award period so that you can make a renewal claim.

Q: What if I think a decision is wrong?

A: You can appeal to an independent Social Security Appeal Tribunal, but must do so within three months of receiving the decision. For appeal procedures relating to all DSS benefits, see **Appendix D, How to Appeal**, at the end of this book.

Q: I am a lone parent but I do receive some maintenance from the child's father. Does this affect my Family Credit entitlement?

A: Maintenance is taken into account when calculating your income, but the first £15 is not counted. If the payments are irregular, the weekly sum will be calculated by working out the average you actually received over the previous 13 weeks.

Q: Will I get any help with my childcare costs?

A: From October 1994, childcare costs of up to £40 a week will be offset against a family's earnings when their Family Credit, Housing Benefit and Council Tax Benefit is calculated, providing there is a child under the age of 11 in the family. This applies to costs incurred with a registered childminder, play scheme or day nursery. This help will be available to two-earner couples, couples where one is incapacitated, and to lone parents.

Q: Does receiving Family Credit help me get any other benefits?

A: Family Credit is a kind of 'passport' to other benefits as receiving this makes you automatically entitled to the following: free NHS prescriptions, free NHS dental treatment, help with the cost of glasses (see **Chapter 7 – How to Collect Free Prescriptions and Other Health Benefits**), and maternity and funeral payments from the Social Fund (see **Chapter 4 – How to Collect Social Fund Loans, Grants and Payments**).

Having covered the main points of Family Credit, we now take a look at the various benefits specifically linked to children. The main one of these is, of course ...

CHILD BENEFIT

Child Benefit – which is paid out in respect of about 12,472,000 children – is a tax-free benefit that is generally payable for all children. It is not means-tested with the result that the amount receivable under this scheme is exactly the same whether you're in the super-tax bracket and live in a millionaire's mansion or are, to use an old-fashioned term, a pauper.

It is the very broad sweep of Child Benefit which has attracted much criticism in recent years with some saying that DSS funds should be allocated more specifically with some reference to 'actual need'. There is little doubt that, of course, a very large part of the £6 billion spent by the Government on Child Benefit ends up in the pockets of families that can hardly be said to really need it. Politicians and pressure groups may continue the debate, but in the meantime for some 6,868,000 families Child Benefit continues to be a very welcome addition to the family budget. Let us now look at some of the details of this very popular benefit.

Who can get it? Child Benefit can be claimed by those who are responsible for children who are: under 16 years of age; aged 16 to 18, but still studying full time; aged 16 or 17 and, having recently left school, are registered for work or training at a careers office. There are some exceptions to this rule and the main ones stop you from getting Child Benefit for a child who is being looked after by a local authority; or if you are the foster parent to a child who is boarded out to you by a local authority; or you and the child (or your husband or wife) have not lived in Great Britain for more than 26 weeks in the past year. If you're excluded because of the last item, you may still qualify straightaway if you start work and begin to pay National Insurance contributions, or come from another EC country to work or from a country which has a reciprocal Social Security agreement with the UK. In those instances, check further with the DSS.

How much do I get? The current rates are £10.20 a week for the oldest qualifying child and £8.25 a week for each other qualifying child. Payment is normally paid four weeks in arrears – either to a bank or building society account or by order book – but you can ask to be paid weekly if you're a lone parent, or either you or your partner are receiving Family Credit, Income Support or Disability Working Allowance and you're being paid by order book.

How do I claim? You can get *leaflet FB8 - Babies and Benefits* from the DSS and use the coupon at the back of it; or get a claim pack from the DSS. You will be asked to send either a birth or adoption certificate with your claim – and the DSS will want to see original documents, not photocopies, but these should be returned to you within a few days. **Important note:** do not delay in claiming because payment can only be backdated for up to six months. If a legal adoption hasn't yet been fully completed, the adoption certificate can be sent later.

Under normal circumstances, the DSS will send you a letter and tell you their decision on your claim. There is an appeals procedure if you disagree with the decision, either because of refusal to pay the benefit or the amount offered.

Child Benefit is one of two weekly cash benefits that can be claimed by a mother under 16. The other one is One-Parent Benefit and now we logically move on to that one ...

ONE-PARENT BENEFIT

One-Parent Benefit is really a kind of topping up of Child Benefit to give additional help to those who are bringing up children on their own. It is, however, paid for the eldest child only.

This tax-free benefit – which is neither means-tested nor dependent on National Insurance contributions – is currently paid to some 937,000 'lone parents', each of whom gets £6.15 a week.

Certain groups are specifically excluded from receiving One-Parent Benefit and you won't be entitled if you are in one of the following groups:

a) You are living with someone as husband and wife (see **Appendix B**).

b) The separation from your partner is a temporary one, such as one of you being in prison or abroad.

c) You are already getting extra money for your eldest or only child as part of one of the following benefits: Widowed Mother's Allowance, War Widow's Pension, Invalid Care Allowance, State Retirement Pension, Unemployability Supplement paid with Industrial Disablement Pension, Industrial Death Benefit at the higher rate for a child (when paid with an Industrial Injuries Widow's Pension).

As the rules covering those who are excluded are quite complex, the DSS recommends that if you're not certain as to whether you qualify you check with their local office.

How to claim. You can get a claim form from your DSS office which should then be sent to: *Child Benefit Centre (Washington), PO Box 1, Newcastle-upon-Tyne NE88 1AA.* Once again, don't delay in claiming as payments can only be backdated for six months. You'll be informed in writing as to what decision has been made.

GUARDIAN'S ALLOWANCE

The Guardian's Allowance is essentially an additional tax-free payment to someone who has taken an orphan into the family. The rate of allowance is £11.00 a week (this being reduced to £9.80 if the beneficiary receives the higher rate of Child Benefit for the same child). This benefit is currently being paid to some 2,000 beneficiaries at an annual cost of about £1 million.

The rules determining who is eligible are quite complicated but you're likely to be entitled if you're looking after a child for whom you're entitled to Child Benefit and one of the following sets of circumstances apply:

a) Both parents of the child are dead.

b) One parent is dead and you cannot trace the surviving one.

c) The parents having divorced, one parent died later and the other parent did not have custody of the child and was not paying maintenance voluntarily and was not liable by court order for maintenance or custody.

d) The child is illegitimate, its mother is dead and its father not known.

e) Under certain circumstances when the surviving parent is in prison.

How to claim. Get *form BG1* from your local DSS office and after completing it return it to that office. Don't delay in claiming as the usual rule about backdating claims for only six months applies. You will be advised in writing about the decision on your claim.

The above completes the section dealing with benefits relating to children. Next we shall look at another important area of 'family' benefits, the one that deals with maternity.

OVERVIEW OF MATERNITY BENEFITS

Major changes are due to take place in maternity benefits in the later part of 1994 to bring the UK in line with the European

Community Directive on the Protection of Pregnant Women at Work. Therefore, this section is divided into two main parts: first, maternity benefits as they apply currently; and, secondly, how the new arrangements will apply to women who are expecting a baby on or after October 16th 1994.

First, the current maternity benefits:

Broadly speaking, there are two principal kinds of maternity benefit available to women through Social Security – and if you are pregnant you might qualify for one or the other, but you can't claim both of these at the same time. Altogether the annual cost of maternity-linked benefits (including those paid by the Social Fund which is covered later) came to an estimated staggering £425 million in 1992/93. Additional to that figure and not included in it are the costs of other benefits, notably: 1) additional benefits in kind paid out to a pregnant woman, such as free milk and free NHS prescriptions; 2) the knock-on effects of maternity benefits on to income-related benefits; and, 3) the costs relating to instances where expectant mothers are receiving incapacity benefits on the grounds of pregnancy-related illnesses. However, most of the money spent in maternity benefits is in the form of compensation paid by the DSS to employers to reimburse them for Statutory Maternity Pay, which is the first of the benefits we now look at in some detail.

STATUTORY MATERNITY PAY

Costing an estimated £420 million in 1993/94, Statutory Maternity Pay (hereafter referred to as SMP) is a weekly payment that pregnant women should be able to claim from their employer, with the amount they get being related to how long they've been working for that employer and also how much they have been earning.

Two tests are applied to find out whether you are eligible for SMP in the first instance. They are:

a) The continuous employment rule: this states that you must have been employed by the same employer for at least 26 weeks into the so-called qualifying week (which is the 26th week of pregnancy or 15 weeks before the week in which your baby is due). If your circumstances match this requirement, the next 'test' to pass is

b) The earnings rule: this states that on average, you must have earned enough to pay Class 1 National Insurance contributions. Average earnings include overtime and any bonuses and it is also important to note that you don't necessarily have had to pay Class 1 NI contributions, but merely earned enough to pay them had you chosen to do so. If you earned enough, but had opted to pay your contributions at the reduced rate available for some married women and widows, you would still qualify.

If your situation satisfies both these rules, you are usually entitled to claim SMP from your employer.

How to claim. You do so by informing your employer that you intend to stop work to have your baby and must, of course, provide evidence that a baby is due – this is usually done by a 'maternity certificate' which should be supplied to you by your doctor or midwife. You should also give your employer at least 21 days notice of the date you intend to stop work. The choice as to when exactly you stop work is essentially yours, but it can affect the number of weeks during which you can get SMP. To get the maximum – which is SMP for 18 weeks – you have to stop work before the start of the 6th week before the week in which the baby is due. Should you choose to work later than this you will end up losing SMP benefit for each week in which you work. The rules governing SMP are complicated and in case of any difficulty you should contact your local DSS office who will be able to advise you.

How much do you get? There are two kinds of SMP payment rates. The first of these – known as Higher Rate SMP – is 90% of your average weekly earnings and is paid for the first six weeks of your entitlement period; thereafter you will get the lower rate. To claim the higher rate you must, when you reach the 'qualifying week', have been employed continuously by the same employer for at least two years, if working full time, or at least five years, if working part time.

If you don't qualify for Higher Rate SMP, you will instead get the lower rate – which is in fact what most SMP claimants get. The rate of payment here is not linked to your earnings but is instead currently a flat £48.80 a week. Once again there is a minimum period of time that you must have been working for the same employer when you reach your qualifying week and this is six months whether you're working full-time or part-time.

How is SMP paid? Normally you will receive your SMP in the same way that you usually received your pay while working. Although the lower rate of SMP is based on a weekly rate, your employer may pay this monthly if your wages were normally paid that way.

When does SMP end? The longest period of time during which you can get SMP is 18 weeks, but under certain conditions it may end earlier than this – for example, if you were to start work for a different employer after the birth of your baby but before the end of the 18-weeks period of SMP. It will also end if you're taken into legal custody or if you were to die.

If you don't qualify for SMP, you may well do so for the next benefit we now look at in some detail.

MATERNITY ALLOWANCE

The purpose of Maternity Allowance – estimated to cost some £43 million in 1993/94 – is to provide benefits for women who are not eligible for SMP, usually because they haven't been working long enough for the same employer before their pregnancy.

Like SMP, Maternity Allowance (hereafter referred to as MA) is payable for a period of 18 weeks, but you will only get this if you meet certain conditions regarding the National Insurance contributions you've paid and you've been either employed or self-employed.

To decide entitlement to MA – which incidentally is one of the few benefits where both the size of the budget and the number of claimants are decreasing – Social Security refer to a 'test period' and this means the period of 52 weeks ending the 15th week before the week in which your baby is due. To qualify for MA, you must have worked and paid standard rate NI contributions for at least 26 weeks of that test period. What's more only standard rate contributions – either as an employee or a self-employed person – paid by you count. Other NI contributions – such as contributions paid for other periods, your husband's contributions, credited contributions or reduced rate contributions paid by some married women and widows – will not help towards satisfying this crucial test.

There are also other reasons why you may not get MA and these include: your baby being stillborn before the 25th week of your pregnancy; if you're sent to prison; or you are living in a non-European Community country or one with which the UK has no reciprocal agreement.

If you pass the contributions hurdle, are not getting SMP from your employer and are not in one of the categories listed above, you may be entitled to MA.

How to claim. There are three different ways to claim MA, depending upon your circumstances:

a) If you're still working for an employer during the 15th week before the expected date of the baby's birth and your employer has refused any application for SMP you may have made, he will give you a form called SMP1 which lists the reasons for not paying you SMP. You should send this SMP1, together with the maternity certificate you would have received earlier from your doctor or midwife, to your local Social Security office together with a Maternity Allowance *claim form MA1*. This last form can be obtained from the DSS office.

b) If you're not working for an employer during the 15th week before the expected date of birth, you should claim by sending the MA1 form and the maternity certificate directly to your DSS office.

c) If you're self-employed, do the same as above, but with one important difference: if you were also employed at any time in the 15th week before the baby is due, you must also provide an SMP1 with your claim to prove that your employer at that time will not pay you SMP. You will also later be asked to prove that you had paid your self-employed NI contributions as required.

If your claim for MA is approved, it is usually paid from the start of the 11th week before the baby is due. The DSS do, however, say "there may be some flexibility as to exactly when the payments start, depending on when you stop work".

How much do you get? There is only one rate of MA, a flat £44.55 a week paid for up to 18 weeks.

UPCOMING CHANGES IN MATERNITY BENEFITS

As explained above, new arrangements affecting both Statutory Maternity Pay and Maternity Allowance are due to come into effect for women expecting a baby on or after October 16th 1994. The main proposals for the new scheme were outlined to the House of Commons on March 8th 1994 and these will be embodied in new regulations to be laid down by the Secretary of State for Social Security.

The key points of the new proposals:

SMP will continue to be paid out by employers for a maximum of 18 weeks and in order to qualify, an expectant mother must:

a) Have 26 weeks of continuous service at her qualifying week – that being the 15th week before her expected week of confinement.

b) Have average earnings at or above the lower earnings limit for the payment of National Insurance contributions.

All women who qualify for SMP under the new proposals will receive:

a) The higher rate (90% of earnings) for the first six weeks of their maternity leave.

b) For the remaining 12 weeks the standard rate of SMP, this being increased to £52.50 to bring it in line with Statutory Sick Pay.

The proposals also include changes in MA – this being paid by the DSS for a maximum of 18 weeks to expectant mothers who cannot get SMP – for which the new qualifying conditions will be that she must have worked and paid at least 26 standard rate National Insurance contributions in the 66 weeks before the week her baby is expected. The new benefit levels for MA will be:

☐ Women who are employed at their qualifying week will receive the same as the new SMP flat rate of £52.50 a week.

☐ Women who are self-employed or who had already given up their job at the qualifying week will get the MA rate of £44.55 a week.

The same starting arrangements will apply to both SMP and MA in that working women will be able to start their maternity benefits at any time from the 11th week before their expected date of confinement right up to the baby's birth. However, if they fall sick with a pregnancy-related illness in the six weeks before the baby is due, their maternity benefit (and leave) will start automatically.

The first payments under the new rules will be made from the end of July 1994.

This brings us to the end of the maternity benefits although there is one more called 'Maternity Payment'. This payment is, however, part of the Social Fund scheme and you'll find details of it in **Chapter 4**.

Additionally, you may also be able to get free milk and vitamins for yourself and your baby – **see Chapter 7 – How to Collect Free Prescriptions and Other Health Benefits**.

And, what's more, while you're looking after a baby or a child under the age of 16, you may be entitled to Home Responsibilities Protection – this is covered in detail at the end of **Chapter 6 – How to Collect Invalidity and Disability Benefits**.

THE CHILD SUPPORT AGENCY

Although not a provider of benefits as such, the recently introduced Child Support Agency (hereafter referred to as CSA) – which is an Executive Agency of the Department of Social Security – can play a major role in determining just how much benefit a lone parent may ultimately get. This happens because the Agency's main task is to ensure the correct assessment as well as the collection from, and payment of child maintenance by, the absent parent to the one who actually has care of the child. Obviously, when the amount of maintenance received from an absent parent increases, the income of the parent with care of the child goes up accordingly. This larger income – subject to any disregard allowed for maintenance – is then taken into account to decide the level of benefits due to the claimant under the new circumstances.

Although the advertisements which accompanied the launch of the CSA left the impression that this was an organisation where single parents could get extra cash help, the reality behind this was that it was the Government's plan to get absent parents to pay as much maintenance as possible as a way of reducing the amount that had to come from Social Security funds. That it was the CSA's main task to save on benefits paid out was clearly spelled out in the agency's first business plan where it acknowledged as one of its aims to provide an "annual benefit saving of £530 million," a target that had been set by the Secretary of State for Social Security.

As has been widely reported since then, the CSA's pursuit of absent parents for maintenance has led to numerous complaints from all kinds of groups. Much of this criticism concerned the way that maintenance was being calculated and the, at times, impossible burden that meeting these payments would place on absent parents. In the face of overwhelming pressure, the Government eventually revised parts of its policy and earlier this year introduced several changes to the way that maintenance would be calculated from early February 1994, all of these changes having the net effect of reducing the amount that absent parents will be expected to pay. It still remains to be seen whether these new levels of maintenance payment will be accepted more readily and to what extent these will affect the CSA's ability to meet its 'savings in benefits' target.

In the meantime, the CSA remains entitled to ask certain Social Security claimants to apply for child support maintenance and this affects all parents with care who get either Income Support, Family Credit or Disability Working Allowance or are the current partner of someone who gets one of these benefits. Anyone falling into one of these categories must apply for an assessment of child support maintenance if requested to do so by the Agency.

People in other categories may apply for child support maintenance assessment – but only if they wish to, as they don't have to. Included in these groups who have the choice are:

☐ Parents with care who are not in receipt of any of the benefits listed above.

☐ People who are not the children's parents, but who have care of the children.

☐ Absent parents.

☐ Children aged 12 or over living in Scotland with at least one parent living apart from them can also apply on their own behalf.

Finally, it needs to be added that the CSA is not only a source of benefits for claimants, but that it, in fact, charges for its services. Currently there are two kinds of standard annual fees:

☐ Annual fee for the assessment and review service – £44, this amount payable by each parent, unless they are receiving Income Support, Family Credit or Disability Working Allowance; or are under the age of 16, or under the age of 19 and in full-time education up to 'A' level or equivalent; or have an income that falls below certain limits.

☐ Annual fee for the collection service – £34. Once again both parents will be expected to pay this amount if either of the parents choose to use the CSA's collection service. There may be exemptions from this charge for parents falling into the groups described above.

If you're not in a category which makes the use of the CSA mandatory, it obviously needs careful consideration whether you would ask them to become involved. For more information, you can ring their Enquiry Line on (0345) 133 133 or pick up a copy of their *booklet CSA 2001 – For Parents Who Live Apart*, which you can get from your DSS office.

3 How To Collect Income Support And Other Social Security Benefits

The previous chapter was primarily concerned with family-linked benefits that applied mostly to people who were in work – or at least in work for more than the 16 hours a week which is the current arbitrary demarcation line that Social Security uses to separate those who are entitled to claim Family Credit and those who are not.

In the first part of this chapter we will look at the major benefit – apart from Unemployment Benefit, Sickness Benefit and Retirement Pensions – which is available to those who are working *less* than 16 hours a week. Further on we will also cover other Social Security benefits, especially those which are available for widows.

But, first of all ....

INCOME SUPPORT

This comparatively new benefit – first introduced in April 1988 – is one of the big spenders of the Social Security programme as it is expected to distribute a staggering £15,773 million this year to provide benefits to an average of more than 5,600,000 beneficiaries at any given time.

The DSS describe it as a benefit to "help people whose income is below a certain level" and that's a fair summing up because Income Support is available to many groups. They further state, and this is worth repeating: "Income Support is paid for out of taxation. If you are eligible for Income Support it is your right to claim it."

Let's begin by looking at the main points of this scheme before examining these in greater detail. First of all, it is an income-related benefit and this means that the amount you can collect will depend upon your financial resources and your savings. Secondly, it is directly related to an individually assessed so-called 'applicable amount' which, of course, can vary greatly according to circumstances.

Subject to your income level and savings, you're likely to be able to get Income Support if you match one of the following categories.

a) You are aged 60 or older.
b) You are unemployed and, to use the standard DSS phrase, available for and actively seeking work.
c) You are unable to work because you're sick or disabled.
d) You can only work part-time, this being defined as less than 16 hours a week.
e) You are a lone parent bringing up a child without the help of a partner.
f) You're unable to go to work because you have to stay at home to look after elderly, sick or disabled relatives.

The above are fundamental conditions of entitlement, but even if you don't belong to one of these groups you may still be eligible if your income is lower than the amount of Income Support you would be entitled to. Incidentally, it is worth noting that your eligibility is not linked to how many – if any – National Insurance contributions you may have paid. However, there is – as with Family Credit – a maximum amount of savings you may have and if these are more than £8,000 for you and your partner (if you have one) you will not get Income Support. Savings of less than £8,000 and more than £3,000 will not disqualify you but will affect the amount you may receive.

How much could you get? The amount of Income Support you could collect is based on a fairly simple principle (although its application can become complicated) which consists of, first of all, working out what your weekly *personal allowances and premiums* are, adding to this certain *housing costs*, including *mortgage interest payments,* that are not covered by Housing Benefit (**see Chapter 11** of this book). The total of all of the foregoing is what is known as your *applicable amount.* What you will get is worked out by making certain deductions from your applicable amount. These deductions would include, among others, any money you or your partner get from any of the following: part-time work, maintenance, certain other Social Security benefits, and so on. What is left after making these deductions from your applicable amount is your entitlement.

Let us now look in greater detail at how the applicable amount is made up. This consists of three main components: **personal allowances, premiums** and **housing costs payments**.

The current weekly personal allowances are: for single people, aged 16 or 17 (if entitled) either £27.50 or £36.15 (the higher figure applies if you have to live away from home under certain circumstances or get the Disability Premium; for single people, 18 to 24, £36.15; or for single people, aged over 18 years and bringing up a child, £45.70; for single people, aged 25 and over, also £45.70; couples, both 18 or over, £71.70. To these amounts of personal allowances are added the following amounts for each child that you're bringing up: for a child under 11, £15.65; a child 11 to 15, £23.00; a child 16 to 17 (subject to certain conditions), £27.50; a child of 18 (also subject to conditions), £36.15.

To these personal allowances are also added the following Weekly Premium amounts for people with children: the **Family Premium** of £10.05 if you have at least one child; the **Disabled Child Premium** of £19.45 if you have a child who is getting Disability Living Allowance or who is registered blind; the **Lone Parent Premium** of £5.10, if you are bringing up one or more children on your own.

There are other Premiums which may apply:

Premiums for **long-term sick or disabled people** – depending on the individual circumstances, these cover a range from £19.45 a week for a single person up to a maximum of £68.60 for a couple.

Premiums for carers are all at the amount of £12.40 for each person to whom it may apply. The **Carer Premium** is added if you or your partner get Invalid Care Allowance or if, from the 1st of October 1990, you or your partner has claimed Invalid Care Allowance but this wasn't paid because the person who claimed it was getting a higher-paying benefit instead.

There are also age-related Premiums:

The **Pensioner Premium** – £18.25 for a single person and £27.55 for a couple. You or your partner have to be 60 to 74 years old to qualify.

The **Enhanced Pensioner Premium** – £20.35 (single); £30.40 (couple). You or your partner have to be aged 75 to 79.

The **Higher Pensioner Premium** – £24.70 (single); £35.30 (couple). Your or your partner have to be over 80. You can also qualify for this premium if you or your partner are 60 or over and one or both of you are getting Attendance Allowance, Disability Living Allowance, Invalidity Benefit, Severe Disablement Allowance or are registered blind.

There is one further list of items that may be added to make up your total applicable amount and that is the one concerned with certain housing costs as some of these are covered by Income Support instead of Housing Benefit (you'll find full details of this benefit in **Chapter 11 – How to Collect Housing Benefit**). The housing costs that help make up your applicable amount can include: the interest portion of your mortgage payments; the interest on loans for essential repairs and improvements to your home; ground rents; hire purchase interest payments if you're buying your home by hire purchase.

As the amounts of money involved here can be very substantial indeed, we will now look at what may or may not be allowed under Housing Costs.

First of all, on mortgage costs it doesn't matter who you have borrowed the money from but it must have been to buy your home. The following conditions also apply:

1) You will not be able to get help with the repayment of capital or with the premiums on an endowment policy or pension that is associated with the loan.

2) There is a limit of £125,000 on the amount of outstanding capital on which Income Support can help you pay the interest. The amount of help that you will get can also be restricted if the Adjudication Officer considers your home as unnecessarily large for you and your family or if it is located in an unnecessarily expensive neighbourhood. However, this restriction cannot be applied for at least six months if you were able to meet the costs when you first moved into your home.

3) You will only receive help with 50% of your eligible interest for the first 16 weeks of your claim if you, and your partner if you have one, are aged under 60. From the 17th week Income Support for mortgage interest is deducted and paid to qualifying lenders automatically.

Income Support may also help with the interest (once again, not repayments of outstanding capital) on loans you had taken out for essential repairs and improvements to your home. The following are likely to be allowed: major repairs to the fabric of the house; damp-proofing; insulation; improvements to drainage; installation of a heating system; putting in a bath or toilet where the accommodation previously lacked suitable facilities; provision of electric sockets and lighting; and 'other reasonable improvements'.

Finally, we come to the part where you can add up all you're entitled to under Income Support and find out what your applicable amount is. Remember, this is made up of: personal allowances plus premiums plus housing costs (if applicable and not covered by Housing Benefit).

From this grand total you will now have to deduct your income and certain amounts relating to capital (for example, savings) in excess of £3,000 that you might have.

We'll deal with the income side first. The money you've got coming in is taken into account on a weekly basis and monthly or yearly amounts are averaged out accordingly.

Income, for this purpose, includes any money you may earn, although a certain part of earnings may be ignored. It also includes most Social Security pensions and benefits although in most cases the following benefits are ignored completely when assessing your entitlement: Housing Benefit, Council Tax Benefit, Attendance Allowance, Christmas Bonus, Constant Attendance Allowance and certain allowances and payments linked to disability or invalidity.

If you have capital over £3,000, the amount of benefit you receive will be affected. For fuller details of this, please refer to **Appendix A – Common Rules** at the back of this book.

It is difficult to work out for yourself just what your exact entitlement under Income Support might be because the rules are complicated by various exceptions. Additionally, there are various regulations to limit the maximum amounts payable for accommodation in special circumstances, such as people in residential or nursing homes, including those who are in such homes because of mental disorders, drug or alcohol dependence, old age, mental handicap or physical disablement. Because of these various permutations, the best thing to do is to work out your applicable amount roughly and make the appropriate deductions for income and capital. If, after doing that, you find that what you've got coming in every week is less than the total of all your allowances, premiums and housing costs, the best thing to do is put in a claim because the chances are that you're entitled to some benefit.

How to claim. Get *leaflet IS1 – Income Support* from your DSS office, fill in the coupon at the back and return it to them. However, if you are unemployed, you have to apply in a different way and you need to get *form B1* from your local Unemployment Benefit office and send that instead to the DSS. Either way, you will then be sent a claim form to fill in with more details of your circumstances. You will also then get a form to claim Housing Benefit and Council Tax Benefit. If you're living in a nursing or residential care home, you can get more information about the special rules affecting you by obtaining DSS *leaflet IS50 – Help if you live in a Residential Care Home or Nursing Home.*

How much do you get? The amounts paid out under Income Support vary tremendously and can range from a few pounds to literally hundreds of pounds a week for someone who is eligible and has a very large mortgage.

QUESTIONS AND ANSWERS ON INCOME SUPPORT

Q: Will my housing costs still be paid if I go away?

A: Generally, yes, but only for a maximum of 52 weeks and then only if it is your intention to return to your house within that period, and only if you have not sub-let the part of your home that you normally live in.

Q: We have two houses with a mortgage on each. Can I claim for both?

A: Yes, you can under certain circumstances. For example, if you had to leave your home because of domestic violence and you are now responsible for payments on two homes. Another acceptable reason might be if one partner of a couple has to live away from home to study or train and the costs of both homes have to be met. You may also be able to claim for two houses for four weeks only when you move and are temporarily responsible for both your old and new homes.

Q: My home is above a shop which I used to run until I had to close it. I qualify for Income Support but my mortgage covers both the flat and the shop. What happens in this case?

A: Help with housing costs will be limited to those which relate to the domestic part.

Q: I am 17 years old and have left my parents' home to live in a flat on my own. Can I get Income Support?

A: There are special rules for determining the Income Support available for those aged 16 or 17. You'll find full details in DSS *leaflet IS26 – Income Support if you are 16 or 17*. Some of the reasons why you might be entitled include: you have no living parents; your relationship with your parents has broken down to the extent you can no longer live with them; you're ill or have a handicap that forces you to live away from home; you're a single parent; you're expecting a baby in less than 11 weeks; you're registered blind; you're a refugee who has been here less than a year and you're learning English.

Q: How long can I get Income Support?

A: The award of Income Support is for an indefinite period of time which means that you'll continue getting it until your circumstances change. It is up to you to tell Social Security of any changes that might affect your entitlement because, if you don't, you may get too much money and may even be breaking the law. If you're in doubt as to whether the DSS has to be informed about a certain change, the safe and sensible thing to do is to tell them anyway.

Q: Do you have to sign on for Income Support?

A: Most claimants have to sign on, but there are exceptions to this: for example, if you're a lone parent and about to have your baby, or if you're looking after a child under 16.

Q: Is maintenance counted as income?

A: Yes, it is. What is more the DSS has a duty to try to make the absent parent of a child living with you pay as much maintenance as possible. And, if you're married to that parent, they will try to ensure that he or she pays you maintenance as well. See the section about the Child Support Agency at the end of the previous chapter.

Q: Will receiving Income Support help me get other benefits?

A: Yes, because if you're getting Income Support you will automatically receive help with the following: the maximum amount of Housing Benefit; the maximum amount of Council Tax Benefit; free prescriptions and other health benefits; free school meals for your children (who may also qualify for a discretionary grant for uniforms from your local education authority). In addition, you will also be entitled to apply to the Social Fund (see **Chapter 4 – How to Collect Social Fund Loans, Grants and Payments**).

For more information get *booklet IS20 – A Guide to Income Support* from your local DSS office.

The above has covered the main points of Income Support and we now turn our attention to another major source of benefits ...

WIDOW'S BENEFITS

Major changes were made in the approach to and the scope of widow's benefits in 1988 and the following information only applies to women who were widowed on or after April 11th 1988. If you were widowed before that date, please see the question and answer section further on.

In the year 1993/94 an average of some 350,000 women are expected to receive widow's benefits at any given time, at a total annual cost of £1,085 million.

Essentially, there are three benefits: Widow's Payment, Widowed Mother's Allowance and Widow's Pension. We will now look at the first of these in some detail.

WIDOW'S PAYMENT

This payment – currently £1,000 for everyone – is a single lump sum that becomes payable immediately when you are widowed. Although the benefit is tax-free, it is however normally dependent upon certain National Insurance contributions conditions.

You should get Widow's Payment if your late husband had met the NI contributions test (see below) or his death was caused by his job (this would include death caused by either industrial accident or disease) and either:

a) You were aged under 60 at the time of his death; or

b) Your husband was not entitled to a Category A Retirement Pension when he died – a Category A pension is the one that is contributory (**see Chapter 15 – How to Collect Retirement Pension** for more details).

There are some exceptions to the above and you won't get Widow's Payment if you are divorced from your husband; or while you may have been living with him as man and wife, you're not legally married to him; or while you are in prison; or you and a man to whom you're not married are living together as husband and wife at the time of your husband's death.

How much do you get? As stated above there is only one payment rate of £1,000. This amount has been the source of much complaint because, unlike most DSS benefits, it hasn't been increased in recent years.

How to claim. As you only have to make one claim for all three Widow's Benefits, this is dealt with at the end of this section.

WIDOWED MOTHER'S ALLOWANCE

The Widowed Mother's Allowance is a regular payment of benefit made up of a basic allowance to which is added an allowance for each of your dependant children. You cannot get Widowed Mother's Allowance and Widow's Pension at the same time. However, should you stop being eligible for the Allowance because you no longer have any dependant children and are still aged under 60, you may then be able to claim Widow's Pension, which is covered later in this section.

The main condition for Widowed Mother's Allowance, providing once again that your late husband has met the NI contributions conditions or if his death was caused by his job, is that your circumstances must match one of the following requirements:

a) You have a child for whom you are entitled to Child Benefit (note that you don't actually have to be getting this benefit, merely entitled to it); or

b) You are expecting your late husband's baby (there are special rules covering a baby you are expecting because of artificial insemination with the semen of someone other than your husband or because of the placing in you of an embryo or of sperm and eggs).

In addition, the child must be either that of yourself and your late husband or a child for whom your husband was entitled to Child Benefit immediately before his death or a child for whom you were entitled to Child Benefit if you and your late husband were living together immediately before his death.

Certain circumstances would stop you from getting the Allowance. These include: if you have been divorced from your husband or if you remarry or while you are living with a man as his wife but without being legally married to him or while you're in prison.

How much do you get? The current rate is £57.60, but there are additions for your children and these are £9.80 for a child for whom the higher rate of Child Benefit is payable; and £11.00 for each other child. On top of that, you may also qualify for Additional Pension (SERPS), covered later in this chapter.

If you don't qualify for Widowed Mother's Allowance, or stop qualifying, you may instead be eligible for ...

WIDOW'S PENSION

This is also a regular weekly payment and like the Widowed Mother's Allowance, it is taxable and depends on meeting NI contributions conditions.

You can get Widow's Pension if your late husband had met the National Insurance contributions requirements or his death was caused by his job and if you meet one of the following conditions as well:
   a) You were aged 45 or over when your husband died and you don't qualify for Widowed Mother's Allowance; or
   b) You are 45 or older when you stop being qualified for the Widowed Mother's Allowance.
The circumstances that would stop you getting Widow's Pension are essentially the same as outlined above in regard to the Widowed Mother's Allowance.

How much do you get? Like Widowed Mother's Allowance, the standard rate for Widow's Pension is £57.60 a week. However, you will only get this if you are at least 55 years old. There are lower rates for younger widows and what you will get depends on your age at the time of your husband's death. These lower rates are – your age is shown first, then the rate: 54 – £53.57; 53 – £49.54; 52 – £45.50; 51 – £41.47; 50 – £37.44; 49 – £33.41; 48 – £29.38; 47 – £25.34 – 46 – £21.31; and 45 – £17.28. You may also be eligible for SERPS which is now explained in some detail.

ADDITIONAL (EARNINGS-RELATED) PENSION (SERPS)

You may be entitled to an Additional Pension on top of either your Widowed Mother's Allowance or Widow's Pension. It is important to note that you may be able to get this extra – known as the State Earnings-Related Pension Scheme or SERPS – even if you don't satisfy the contribution conditions for the basic allowance or pension.

You should be able to get this additional pension if you meet the following two conditions:
   a) Your husband must have died on or after April 6th 1979; and
   b) He must have paid standard rate NI contributions as an employee since April 1978 on earnings between the so-called lower and upper earnings limits applicable at the time. Class 2 contributions – as a self-employed person – will also be taken into account.

How much do you get? The amount is highly variable as it depends on a very complicated formula which takes into account the following factors: your late husband's earnings for each tax year, except the one which ended on April 5th before he died; increases in line with the rise in national average earnings, this increase being approved by Parliament each year; and what was the 'qualifying level' of earnings for Basic Pension in the last complete tax year before the one in which your husband died, as this amount is taken away from each of his revalued earnings. If this calculation leaves a surplus amount of earnings, that is the amount that is taken into account each year towards Additional Pension.

There is one more part to the formula and that is that the 'total surplus' is divided by 80, then divided again by 52 to provide the weekly rate payable – which may range from a few pounds to considerably more. There are also special conditions which reduce the amount of Additional Pension in the case of a widow whose husband had been a member of a contracted-out pension scheme or who had taken out a personal pension instead of the Additional Pension.

If is worth stressing that you may still be entitled to SERPS even if your late husband was self-employed while he was in the scheme because each Class 2 NI contribution he paid (the self-employed 'stamp') is counted as though it had been a Class 1 contribution at the lower earnings limit.

How to claim. Although the rules governing Widow's Benefits are complex, the good news is that at least they're relatively easy to claim as you do not have to make a claim for each benefit separately and one claim form – *BW1* – automatically covers the lot. When you register your husband's death, you will be given a special death certificate which is for DSS use only. This death certificate – after you've filled in the details on the back of it – should then be sent or taken to your DSS office. Soon thereafter you should receive the actual claim form BW1 which, of course, needs to be completed and returned to the DSS, together with your birth certificate, your husband's birth certificate and your marriage certificate. If you haven't got all of these immediately at hand, they can be supplied later. Whatever you do, don't delay making a claim because claims usually can't be backdated for more than a year and only six months for increases for children.

QUESTIONS AND ANSWERS ON WIDOW'S BENEFITS

Q: What are the NI contributions conditions referred to above?
A: Very broadly speaking – because the actual rules are complicated and contain various exceptions and qualifications – your husband's NI contribution record must meet the following condi-

tions: For **Widow's Allowance** (see next question for more details of this) or **Widow's Payment** – either, before April 6th 1975, he must have paid at least 25 Class 1, 2 or 3 contributions before age 65 or after April 6th 1975, he must have paid contributions in any one year for at least 25 times the lower earnings limit for that year. A different set of rules applies for **Widowed Mother's Allowance** and **Widow's Pension** and for you to qualify, your husband once again must have met a set minimum of NI contributions or have paid 50 flat-rate contributions at any time before April 6th 1975. There is a second test which relates to the amount you will actually get (which could be less than 100% of the standard rate) which concerns the number of years that his contributions met the conditions.

Q: Why are the rules different for women who were widowed before April 11th 1988?

A: That was the date when a major reform of Social Security benefits took place and the Widow's Benefit Scheme was changed as well. Women widowed before then were entitled – subject to qualifying conditions, of course – to the Widow's Allowance which was a regular payment for 26 weeks. There wasn't, however, any Widow's Payment and the conditions for Widowed Mother's Allowance and Widow's Pension were somewhat different.

For more detailed information, you can consult *booklet NP45 – A Guide to Widow's Benefits* which you can get from your local DSS office and which also contains more information about the current benefits.

Apart from the benefits for widows described above, there is one more, the War Widow's Pension, full details of which you'll find in **Chapter 13 – How to Collect War Pensions and Benefits**. The last benefit to be covered in this chapter is ...

THE CHRISTMAS BONUS

This tax-free bonus is automatically sent to you – either with your benefit or as a separate payment – if, during the 'qualifying week' which is the week beginning with the first Monday in December, you are entitled to one of the following benefits:

Retirement Pension, a Widow's Benefit, Attendance Allowance, Invalid Care Allowance, Disability Living Allowance, Invalidity Pension, Severe Disablement Allowance, Income Support (but you also have to be over pension age), War Widow's Pension and certain other benefits.

How much do you get? The current rate is £10 for everyone who qualifies. However, you will only get one bonus, no matter how many times you qualify because you're receiving several different benefits. Nice though the idea is of a Christmas bonus, it has been attacked as being a touch Scrooge-like because it hasn't been increased for many a year.

4 How To Collect Social Fund Loans, Grants And Payments

The Social Fund provides a strange mixture of benefits. The DSS describe it as a way of helping people "with expenses which are difficult to meet from their regular income" and the fund seeks to do this with three different kinds of benefits: loans, grants and payments.

The obvious difference between these is that you would be expected to repay a loan whereas that normally would not apply with grants or payments. There are other differences, however, and that is that payments are made according to the law and decisions on these payments are made by Adjudication Officers, which means that if you meet the conditions imposed by law, you will receive your payment.

Things are not quite so simple with loans and grants because the decision whether or not to grant these rests with a Social Fund Officer. He is, of course, bound by directions and considers guidance to decide who is eligible and how much they should get. But, after considering all these aspects, the final decision takes into account one more factor – and that's how much money there is currently in the local kitty. If the Fund is low on money, you'll have to present a much stronger case to get a loan or a grant; on the other hand, should the fund be flush with cash (an unlikely occurrence, we may add), even comparatively low priority applicants may get their requests granted.

The system works like this: Social Security offices are given two budgets each year, one for grants and one for loans, and Social Fund Officers are not allowed to overspend these budgets. So, the decision as to who gets what is influenced by how much money there is at hand and the DSS's assessment of your circumstances because they are briefed to "meet the needs of the most vulnerable local people who are in the greatest difficulty" first. What this means in practice is that if a Social Fund Officer decides that there are cases more needy than yours, your application may well be turned down if funds are low.

Let us begin by looking first at the two kinds of loans available which in the current year are estimated to be made available to some 1,529,000 beneficiaries at a total cost of £40 million, which works out to an average of just over £26 each. Incidentally, it is worth noting that while the budget for most DSS benefits increases every year, the one for the Social Fund is actually decreasing. For example, two years ago, it was estimated that there would be 1,287,000 beneficiaries at a total cost of £52 million, or £12 million more than now. What's more, at that time the average payment worked out at about £40 each.

SOCIAL FUND BUDGETING LOANS

A Budgeting Loan is an interest-free loan which is intended to help people spread the cost of one-off expenses over a longer period.

To qualify for a Budgeting Loan, you or your partner must have been receiving Income Support for at least 26 weeks although a gap in this of up to 14 days is ignored. How much you get will depend on the cost of your intended purchase, whether that amount is considered reasonable and whether you are able eventually to repay this. The amount will, however, never exceed £1,000 or be for less than £30.

You can apply for a loan for almost any reasonable purpose but it is more likely to be granted for high priority items which include: *essential items of furniture, bedclothes, household equipment; removal expenses* if your move is essential; *electric and gas meter installations and reconnection charges;* certain other *fuel costs.* Next on the list are medium priority items such as non-essential furniture; redecoration; hire purchase and other debts; clothing. Lowest on the list are low priority items which include: rent in advance or removal expenses if the move is not essential; leisure items (such as a radio or television).

As stated earlier, no interest is added to a Budgeting Loan, but you will be required to pay back an agreed amount each week. How much you have to pay back weekly will depend upon the size of the loan and your other commitments – for example, other loans or fuel bills you have outstanding. Usually, the loan will have to be paid back at a rate of between 5 and 15 pence for every pound of Income Support you get over a period of up to 18 months.

The DSS do stress that each application is judged on its own merits and there are no hard and fast rules. For example, money for a vacuum cleaner would normally not qualify as a high priority item, but it might well do so if someone in your household was severely allergic to dust.

How to apply. See end of this chapter.

SOCIAL FUND CRISIS LOANS

Crisis Loans are quite different from Budgeting Loans as you don't have to be getting Income Support – or, for that matter, any kind of Social Security Benefit – to be able to apply for one. Whether or not you might be able to get one will depend upon how the Social Fund Officer at your local office gauges your circumstances and decides whether you or your family would suffer without a Crisis Loan, no matter what your normal source of income might be. The other consideration taken into account here is also the state of the Social Fund as there has to be enough money available.

The DSS say: "We can only usually give a Crisis Loan when it is the only way to prevent a serious risk of damage to health or safety. We have given Crisis Loans when people have lost money, lost things in a fire or been stranded away from home." Remember that these are only examples and you can still apply if your circumstances are other than those described.

The DSS further point out that a Crisis Loan is intended to provide help over a period of crisis although it may not necessarily solve the crisis altogether. There is a top limit of £1,000, but there is no minimum.

Crisis Loans are repayable and the repayment arrangements are similar to those for Budgeting Loans (see above). However, you would not be expected to start repayments until the crisis is over.

There are some categories of people who are not eligible for Crisis Loans and these include: someone aged under 16, a resident of a nursing home or residential care home, anyone who is detained under the law, a hospital in-patient, a full-time student.

Neither are you likely to be able to get a Crisis Loan if help should be forthcoming from your local council instead as they are responsible for dealing with disasters in their area. Disasters include those which affect only a single house (such as a gas explosion) to those which cover a much wider area (such as floods or chemical spillages).

How to apply. See end of this chapter.

The above covers the loans available through the Social Fund. We will now look at the one form of grant ...

SOCIAL FUND COMMUNITY CARE GRANTS

These grants benefit some 338,000 applicants a year at a total cost of £96 million – which works out to an average of £284 per grant. And, of course, unlike the benefits listed above, they don't have to be repaid. Once again, this is an area where the number of expected beneficiaries has gone up and although the budget for this benefit has been increased it has only been done so enough to allow for an expected average grant that is some £9 less than it was two years ago.

One of the main intentions of **Community Care Grants** (hereafter called CCG) is to help people in particular groups, such as the elderly and the disabled, to live independently in the community. Although that is the main aim, the actual scope is somewhat wider and includes as well help for people leaving institutional or residential care, families under exceptional pressure and, occasionally, assistance with travelling costs.

To be eligible for a CCG, you must be receiving Income Support in the first place. There are, however, exceptions to this if you are coming out of institutional care.

The sort of things that CCGs have been granted for vary considerably and here's a partial list:

For *people coming out of hospital, prison or other care* – help with furniture, bedclothes, removal and connected expenses.

For families under exceptional pressure, such as a *long-term illness* or *family breakdown* – help with clothing, furniture, payment for moving costs after the break-up of a relationship.

To *enable people to continue living in their own home* (especially if they are handicapped or disabled in any way) – help may be available for things like a microwave oven for someone who can't use a cooker safely, a washing machine for someone with a heavy burden of laundry, extra bedding for a bedbound person, a food processor for someone who can't swallow solid food.

Travelling expenses – these may be paid, for example, to visit someone who is ill, to attend a relative's funeral, help ease a domestic crisis, or visit children staying with the other parent before a custody decision.

The above are only a broad overview of the sort of things for which a CCG may be given as each case is judged on its merits. Grants have been given for many other purposes – such as alterations to stairs for a disabled person or minor structural repairs to make a home safe for a child. The short answer is ask anyway if you think there is a remote chance that you qualify.

Whether you get a grant at all will also depend upon your own financial circumstances, and these will affect whether you get the whole amount, or only part of it.

How to apply. See the end of this chapter.

The next part of the Social Fund we will now look at concerns 'payments'. The first one of these is ...

SOCIAL FUND MATERNITY PAYMENTS

This is a nice straightforward benefit with comparatively simple rules for eligibility and one single payment – £100 – being payable. It was claimed last year by some 226,400 mothers at a total cost of nearly £23 million.

Because it is a 'payment', you will get this if you qualify no matter what the state of the Social Fund budget. To be eligible you, or your partner, must be getting Income Support, Family Credit or Disability Working Allowance. Additionally, you may also get this payment if you're adopting a baby and the baby is not more than a year old when you apply.

There is one small catch: the amount of Maternity Payment you get is affected by your savings as your payment will be reduced on a pound for pound basis by any savings you or your partner have over £500 (this amount is increased to £1,000 if you or your partner are aged 60 or older). There are time limitations on putting in your claim and you must do this between 11 weeks before your baby is due to three months after the birth. In the case of adoptions, the claim must be made within three months after adopting the baby.

Claiming Maternity Payment will have no effect on any other benefits you may already be receiving.

How to apply. See end of this chapter.

SOCIAL FUND FUNERAL PAYMENTS

The conditions for being eligible for a Funeral Payment are somewhat different. You should be able to claim this if you or your partner are responsible for arranging a funeral and don't have enough to pay for it and if you're already in receipt of any of the following benefits: Income Support, Family Credit, Disability Working Allowance, Housing Benefit or Council Tax Benefit.

Some 67,000 beneficiaries a year receive a Funeral Payment at a total cost of £57 million, or about £850 each on average. How much you may get is affected by:

a) What money may be available from the deceased person's estate.

b) Any money that may be available from insurance policies, payments by a pension scheme and other such sources.

c) Any savings you or your partner have over £500 (£1,000 if either of you is over 60 years of age).

The Funeral Payment will help towards what the DSS calls a 'simple funeral' and this is likely to include: the cost of bringing the body home, or to an undertaker; travel costs to arrange the funeral or to attend it (one return journey only); the cost of the death certificate; an ordinary coffin or urn; flowers from the person arranging the funeral; fees (for chaplain, undertaker and organist); cemetery or crematorium costs; and extra costs up to £75 if these costs are incurred because of the religion of the deceased person.

You have to apply for a Funeral Payment within three months of the date of the funeral and this payment won't affect any other benefits you get.

How to apply. See end of this chapter.

Finally, we come to the last Social Fund benefit ...

SOCIAL FUND COLD WEATHER PAYMENTS

This is a payment that is made automatically as a lump sum to those who are eligible to help with extra heating costs during extremely cold weather.

The payment of £7 a week comes into effect if the average daily temperature for your area is 0 degrees Celsius (freezing point or 32 degrees Fahrenheit) or colder over a continuous seven-day period. The payment is also made when such a spell of cold weather has been forecast by the Meteorological Office. It's worth noting that this payment – which previously had been £6 a week – was increased to its new level to partially offset the extra heating costs resulting from the imposition of VAT on domestic fuels. When the increase was announced at the end of 1993, the Government added that it was also intended that there would be a further increase to £7.50 in time for the 1995/96 winter.

To qualify, you or your partner must be getting Income Support which includes as well either a premium for being over 60 years of age, or one for being disabled or long-term sick. You may also qualify if your Income Support includes an amount for a child under five.

Two pieces of good news about these payments: first of all, they are not affected by any savings you might have, and, secondly, there is no need to make a claim to receive them as the DSS will automatically send them to those who qualify. This is a big improvement over previous years when you had to watch for claim forms to appear in the Press whenever there had been very cold weather. For more information, see: DSS *leaflet CWP1 – Extra help with heating costs when it's very cold.*

HOW TO APPLY FOR SOCIAL FUND BENEFITS

Here's how to claim Social Fund Benefits:

Budgeting Loans and Community Care Grants: *Form SF300* which you can get from your local DSS office.

Crisis Loans: There is no form and you should call at your local DSS office for an interview where your application will be dealt with by a Social Fund Officer. If you're away from home when the crisis occurs, contact the nearest DSS office. Some time thereafter, you will receive a letter letting you know the decision that has been reached. If you are offered a loan, the letter will state the amount of it and at what rate you're expected to repay it. The DSS will ask you to sign this letter to acknowledge the repayment terms.

Maternity Payments: You claim on *Form SF100* which you can get either from the DSS or your antenatal clinic. See also DSS *leaflet FB8 – Babies and Benefits.*

Funeral Payments: Use *Form SF200*, available from the DSS or local Registrar of Births, Deaths and Marriages. See also DSS *leaflet D49 – What to do after a death.*

49

5   How To Collect Sickness Benefits

Benefits for people who are sick have been one of the mainstays of the Welfare State since its inception and this remains one of the main areas of spending. Major changes have, however, been proposed in two of the benefits – Sickness Benefit and Invalidity Benefit – from April 1995 when they may both be replaced by a new benefit tentatively called 'Incapacity Benefit'. For more details of these proposed changes, see the special note at the end of the next chapter.

Essentially, the DSS broadly divides those who cannot work because of illness into two groups – those whose unfitness for work lasts less than 28 weeks and those who are unfit for longer than that. In this chapter, we shall look at the provisions for the comparatively short-term sick.

There are two main short-term provisions for people who are sick, Statutory Sick Pay (SSP) and Sickness Benefit (SB). The main difference is that the former is for employees only.

STATUTORY SICK PAY

SSP is paid by employers to qualifying employees who are off sick from work. Employers used to be reimbursed eight per cent of their SSP costs but this reimbursement was abolished from April 6th 1994.

Here's how SSP works out in practice.

First of all, you have to be sick for at least four days in a row. For this purpose, all days are counted including weekends, holidays or days that you would normally have off. SSP is, however, only paid for so-called 'qualifying days' and these can be any days agreed between you and your employer and they are usually the days of the week that you are required by your contract to be available for work. For example, if you usually work from Monday to Friday then these five contractual days would normally be 'qualifying days', while Saturday and Sunday would not. If you do not have to work in a particular week, then the Wednesday of that week becomes the qualifying day. SSP is not payable for the first three qualifying days in a spell of sickness – these being called 'waiting days'.

There is one more important condition that you must satisfy to get SSP and that is that you must have earned enough to have paid National Insurance contributions. This means that your total average pay, before deductions, during the eight weeks before your illness must have been sufficient for you to have paid NI contributions. Currently, you have to pay these if you earn more than £57 a week.

If you meet these conditions, you should be entitled to SSP, but there are exceptions (see Questions and Answers below).

How to get SSP: You or someone acting on your behalf must inform your employer that you are sick, either by telephone or letter or possibly both. Some employers have particular rules about how they want their employees to notify them of sickness so you need to find this out from your employer. It is also important for you to find out what kind of evidence of your sickness your employer wants you to provide. If your absence from work is for less than seven days (including Sundays) you will normally be required to complete a self-certification form for your employer which can be either *form SC2* (which is produced by the DSS) or a form produced by your employer. If your absence is for more than seven days your employer may ask you to provide medical evidence.

There is one more important rule governing SSP and this states that any spells of sickness of four or more days in a row with eight weeks or less between them are linked and counted as one spell. This means that under those circumstances you will not have to serve another three waiting days. However, if your previous spell of sickness was with another employer you will have to serve another three waiting days.

How much do you get? Currently there are two rates of SSP: for those with gross weekly earnings of £200 or more – £52.50; for earnings between £57 and £199.99 – £47.80. SSP is payable for up to 28 weeks in a period of sickness although this may be reduced if your period of sickness links to a previous period of sickness with the same or a previous employer.

QUESTIONS AND ANSWERS ON STATUTORY SICK PAY

Q: Who are the exceptions referred to earlier who cannot get SSP?

A: You will not get SSP if – on the first day of sickness – you are a serving member of the Armed Forces; or are a foreign-going mariner; or have a short-term contract of three months or less; or have not yet done any work for your employer; or are outside the European Economic Area (EEA); or are in legal custody; or are away from work because of a trade dispute; or are within the 'disqualifying period' if you are pregnant or have just had a baby; or are over pension age or under the age of 16; or have already had 28 weeks of SSP from your previous employer and you fall sick again within eight weeks of receiving your last SSP from your previous employer; or your current sickness links with a claim to Social Security benefit; or your earnings do not attract a liability for National Insurance contributions.

Q: My employers tell me that they have their own sick pay scheme. How does that work?

A: Entitlement conditions for occupational sick pay are a matter between the employer and their employees and not something over which the Department of Social Security has any control. However, if SSP is due for a day, and the employer is already paying occupational sick pay for that day, the employer's liability is met by this payment of occupational sick pay, provided that it is equal to or greater than the SSP due.

Q: Does my sick note have to be signed by a doctor?

A: No, not necessarily, although that is the usual way. If you are being treated by someone other than a doctor or a hospital – such as an osteopath, acupuncturist or other practitioner – a note from them might be accepted by your employers instead. If they choose not to accept this as evidence, you may ask your local DSS office whether you should be paid. The short answer is to play safe and, if at all possible, get a sick note from a doctor or hospital.

Q: How is SSP paid?

A: You will normally be paid SSP by your employers in the same way as you received your pay and the usual deductions, such as National Insurance and tax, will be made from it.

Q: What happens if I change jobs while I am sick?

A: You get *form SSP1 (L)* – called a 'leaver's statement' – from your old employer and give this to your new employer when you start your new job.

Q: Are part-time workers entitled to SSP?
A: You may be able to get SSP for those days which are 'qualifying days', that is days when you would have been expected to have worked had you not been sick.

Q: What happens with people who have more than one job?
A: You could get more than one amount of SSP if you qualify with each employer separately.

Q: What do I do if I don't agree with my employer's decision?
A: Get in touch with your local DSS office and ask for a formal Adjudication Officer's decision on the matter.

For more information. See *leaflet NI244 – Statutory Sick Pay – Check Your Rights*, available from the DSS.

If you don't qualify for SSP, you may be able to get instead ...

SICKNESS BENEFIT

This is the alternative benefit, as it were, because it covers many of those who fall outside the safety net provided by SSP. In 1992/93, this benefit was being paid to an average of 135,000 claimants at any given time at a total annual cost of £315 million.

Sickness Benefit (hereafter referred to as SB) is available to eligible people who fall into one of the following categories:
a) If you're an employee and incapable of work because of sickness, but you cannot get SSP from your employer; or
b) You are self-employed, unemployed or non-employed.

However, to receive SB you must also have paid enough Class 1 (employee) or Class 2 (self-employed) National Insurance contributions at the right time and you must satisfy both of the following conditions:
a) You must have qualifying earnings relating to Class 1 and/or Class 2 contributions actually paid in any one tax year equal to at least 25 times the weekly lower earnings limit for that year. Alternatively, you will meet this first condition if you have paid 26 flat-rate Class 1 and/or Class 2 contributions before April 6th 1975. It is important to note that for this condition, 'credits' of contributions do not count, you need to have paid actual contributions; and

b) You must also have qualifying earnings relating to Class 1 and/or Class 2 contributions actually paid or Class 1 credits equal to 50 times the weekly lower earnings limit in both of the two relevant tax years. In this instance, however, 'credits' do count and you may have received these for each complete week – that is a Monday to Saturday inclusive – when you were previously sick and unable to work or you were unemployed. It is further important to note that the reduced rate contributions paid by some married women and widows do not count for SB purposes.

There is an exception to the above and that is that if your inability to work is because of an accident at work, or because you have an industrial disease, you will be treated as having satisfied the contribution condition.

Generally, you won't be allowed to do any work while you are registered as being sick, but there are some exceptions to this, for example, work done under medical supervision for rehabilitation purposes and for which you earn less than £43.00 a week. If you plan to do this kind of work – called 'therapeutic work' – be sure to tell your local DSS office about it first and they will be able to say whether this is likely to affect your benefit in any way.

How to claim. The procedure for claiming SB is somewhat complicated as there are two possible ways to go about it.

If you're **employed** – and you either are not entitled to SSP or it runs out and you are still ill – your employer will send you *form SSP1* which, first of all, tells you why and how much SSP, if any, has been paid to you to date. With this form you will also automatically receive a claim form for Sickness Benefit as well as any sick note that you may have given your employer in the first instance. You should complete the SSP1 form as soon as possible and send it, together with any sick note you may have, to your local DSS office. As usual, the advice is that you should not delay because you could lose benefit if you do.

The procedure for claiming is different from the above if you're either **self-employed, unemployed or non-employed** and what you should do is to get *form SC1* (this is usually available from doctors' surgeries, hospitals or your DSS office). Fill in this form – which is accepted as evidence of your illness for up to six days, not counting Sundays – and send it immediately to your DSS office.

As with SSP, you will not get Sickness Benefit for the first three 'waiting days', but there are exceptions to this rule as you will get it in either of the following two situations:

a) If you were getting Sickness Benefit or were due for SSP at any time in the eight weeks before your claim you won't have to serve out the three waiting days; or

b) If your SSP stopped just as you were about to return to work you can get SB for less than four days.

There are also special rules for those who need regular medical treatment and cannot work two or three days in six consecutive days and they may be able to get benefit for the days that they can't work. Treatments covered by this include regular dyalisis, radiotherapy, chemotherapy by cytotoxic drugs and plasmapheresis.

Your self-certificate of sickness is effective only for a week. If you're ill longer than that you will have to get a sick note from your doctor or hospital – and keep getting these – until you get one that states a date when you will be fit to go back to work. Fill in the back of these notes and send them immediately to the DSS, making sure that there is no gap in the dates of the sick notes because that might cause you to lose money.

If by chance you are given a sick note which is not on one of the standard three forms – *Med 3*, *Med 5* or *Med 10* – send the note to the DSS with a letter to say that you're claiming benefit.

How much do you get? That depends on your age. If you're under pension age, the current weekly rate is £43.45; if you're over pension age, it's £55.25.

In addition, you may be able to claim for dependant adults and children. For full details, see **Appendix C** at the back of this book.

QUESTIONs AND ANSWERS ON SICKNESS BENEFIT

Q: Can I get Sickness Benefit at the same time as other benefits?

A: Yes and no – it depends on what the other benefit is. You can't get SB as well as Unemployment Benefit, Retirement Pension, Maternity Allowance, unemployability supplement of any kind, a training allowance of any kind, Statutory Sick Pay and Statutory Maternity Pay. However, you can get SB at the same time as Disability Living Allowance as a severely disabled person or as well as a basic War or Industrial Injuries Disablement Pension or gratuity.

Q: What happens if my employer continues to pay my wages?

A: This has no effect and you can still claim SB.

Q: What happens if I go into hospital for a long period?

A: If you go into hospital (that is either an NHS hospital or another where maintenance is provided from public funds), your Sickness Benefit will be reduced after six weeks of free in-patient treatment. Extra benefits for dependants may also be affected if the dependant goes into hospital (for more information on this, get DSS *leaflet NI9 – Going into hospital?*).

Q: What do I do about my National Insurance contributions while I'm sick?

A: As a general rule, there's no need to do anything as you will usually get a contribution credit for each full week (in this instance that means Monday to Saturday) while you're sick. However, you won't get these credits if you're only sick for part of a week unless you're unemployed for the rest of that week; or you are a married woman paying the reduced rate stamp; or for any weeks in or after the tax year during which you reach pension age.

Q: How long can I get SB?

A: It is paid for 28 weeks, but if you're still ill at the end of that period you will automatically become eligible for invalidity benefit which is dealt with in the next chapter of this book.

For more information. See *leaflet NI16 – Sickness Benefit*, available from the DSS.

6 How To Collect Invalidity And Disability Benefits

The previous chapter has dealt with benefits available for people who are sick for up to six months, or more exactly up to 28 weeks. If you're still sick and unable to work when your entitlement to Sickness Benefit or Statutory Sick Pay comes to an end, you usually go on to Invalidity Benefit which we will now cover in some detail.

INVALIDITY BENEFIT

This tax-free benefit was claimed by an average of some 1,600,000 beneficiaries at any given time during 1993/94 at a total cost of more than £6,697 million.

Invalidity Benefit (hereafter referred to as IB) is made up of four separate components of which the most important one is the basic invalidity pension itself, because if you don't qualify for that one, you won't get any of the other components either. The components – and how you qualify for each – are:

a) *Basic Invalidity Pension.* To be entitled to this you must previously have been entitled, or have been treated as though you were, to 28 weeks of Sickness Benefit in a period of interruption of employment. Entitlement to Maternity Allowance will also count. The other way you can qualify is that if you were an employee who was entitled to Statutory Sick Pay for 28 weeks, providing that you had satisfied the contribution conditions for Sickness Benefit when you first got SSP. However, if you received less than 28 weeks of SSP, you will have to receive Sickness Benefit until the total of 28 weeks is reached. It is important to note that the 28 weeks of entitlement do not all have to be one after the other, as periods of interruption of employment which are not more than eight weeks apart are counted as one period – the so-called 'linking' effect. If you qualify for the basic pension, you will continue to get it for as long as you remain unable to work in that period of interruption or until you reach pensionable age.

How much do you get? The current weekly rate is £57.60.

b) *Additional Invalidity Pension.* This is an increase on the basic IP and depends on your earnings between April 1978 and April 1991 on which you paid Class 1 (employed) National Insurance contributions.

How much do you get? The amount is quite variable as your individual National Insurance contributions set the level which you would be paid.

c) *Invalidity Allowance.* Whether you get this depends upon your age. You will be eligible for this supplement if you were under the age of 60 (for men) or under the age of 55 (for women) on your first day of incapacity for work in the period of interruption of employment and this also includes days when you were getting SSP.

How much do you get? There are three rates and the one you get is related to your age on the first day of incapacity (not your age now). The scales are: higher rate of £12.15 weekly for those aged under 40; the middle rate of £7.20 for those aged 40 to 49; and the lower rate of £3.80 for men aged 50 to 59 and women aged 50 to 54.

d) *Extra Benefits for Dependants.* You may also be able to get extra benefit for an adult dependant and your children. **See Appendix C** at the back of this book for fuller details of what these payments may be and how they can be affected by the earnings of those dependants.

How to claim. Claim in the same way as Sickness Benefit (see previous chapter), although generally you won't get Invalidity Benefit at that stage because you won't have satisfied the 28 week rule. However, if you've had previous spells of illness which can be 'linked' together, you may get IB from the start of your claim. If you qualify for IB while you're getting Sickness Benefit – or after 28 weeks of SSP – the DSS will pay the new benefit automatically. Once you've started to receive IB, you will have to keep sending sick notes from your doctor as long as you're still too ill to work so as to continue your claim.

There are special rules covering the availability of IB for widows and widowers who are too ill to work and these mainly relate to the age of the surviving spouse at the time of the death of their partner. They also allow – under certain circumstances – that the rate of IB they receive will be based upon their late spouse's NI contributions rather than their own as they will get whichever produces the higher amount.

For more information. Get *leaflet NI16A – Invalidity Benefit* from your local DSS office.

As you will have seen, your right to IB is very dependent upon your National Insurance contributions record which means that many very long-term sick people don't qualify. It was to cater for these groups that the next benefit was created ...

SEVERE DISABLEMENT ALLOWANCE

Received by some 322,000 beneficiaries in 1992/93 at a total cost of £686 million, this Allowance (hereafter referred to as SDA) is tax-free money paid to people who either have never been able to work or who have not been able to work for at least 28 weeks because of physical or mental illness or disability. A further qualification for SDA is that the recipients are ineligible for either Sickness Benefit or Invalidity Benefit because they haven't paid enough NI contributions – although, if they get SDA, they will be credited with contributions.

The benefit is not means-tested in any way whatsoever and it doesn't matter how much money you might have. To qualify, you must, first of all, meet one of the two following conditions:

a) You must have become incapable of work on or before your 20th birthday; or

b) If your incapacity started after your 20th birthday, you have to be at least 80% disabled (this is explained further on).

Additionally, you also have to have been incapable of work for at least 28 weeks – this is called the 'qualifying period' – and you must be at least 16 years of age, but under 65. However, you can continue receiving SDA after the age of 65 if you were receiving it the day before you reached that age.

Unless you qualified automatically because you were incapable of work before your 20th birthday, the question of how disabled you are is most important as you need to be at least 80% disabled to qualify. Here are some guidelines to help you assess whether you might qualify.

Some people are accepted without the need for further medical evidence as being 80% disabled on the basis of other benefits they may already be receiving and you might qualify on this basis if you: get the middle or higher rate of Disability Living Allowance; or get the war pensioner's mobility supplement; or are registered as blind or partially-sighted; or have received an award under the vaccine damage payments scheme; or have in the past been assessed as being 80% disabled under the industrial injuries or war pensions schemes, so long as the period covered by that original assessment has not yet expired.

If, however, you don't meet any of the conditions that allow the DSS to 'accept' you as being sufficiently disabled, you will have to undergo a medical examination to assess the extent of your disablement. This assessment takes into account all of your disabilities as two or more may add up to give the required 80% whereas one might not have sufficed. All and any types of illnesses and disabilities – whether physical or mental – are taken into account. Says the DSS: "In general, if your overall condition is such that you are severely restricted in the things you can do, or you cannot lead a normal life, you may be well regarded as 80% disabled."

Each case is assessed individually and it is therefore impossible to give hard and fast examples. However, some disabilities have a fixed percentage and these are listed in the Schedule of Prescribed Degrees of Disablement. Here are some examples: loss of both hands – 100%; loss of a hand and a foot – 100%; loss of sight to such an extent as to make you incapable of work for which sight is essential – 100%; absolute deafness – 100%; amputation through shoulder joint – 90%; amputation of both feet – 80%; loss of a hand or of the thumb and four fingers of one hand – 60%; loss of three fingers from one hand – 30%; loss of one eye, the other being normal – 40%; very severe facial disfiguration – 100%.

Unlisted disabilities are assessed in two ways: by comparing the effects of your disability with those listed and also by comparing your mental or physical condition with that of a non-disabled person of the same age and sex. The DSS provided the following example: "If you have such bad arthritis in your hand that you cannot use it at all, you may be assessed as if you had actually lost your hand (60% disablement). If you have pain, the assessment may be higher."

Even more difficult to assess are cases of learning difficulties or mental illness. After building up as complete a picture as possible of the applicant from doctors' reports, hospital casenotes, social services and so on, the assessor will take into account other relevant factors which might include: to what extent can the disabled person look after themself without outside help; or how he or she may spend the day; or how much he or she understands and responds to the surrounding people and things. The DSS points out, however:

"A disabled person who is capable of carrying out all the functions of everyday living unaided, but can only do so when instructed and prompted may well be assessed as 100% disabled. In many cases, of course, the person with learning difficulties will have had the condition since birth and will not have to satisfy the 80% condition."

How much do you get? The amount you receive each week will vary according to when you first became incapable of work because of your illness. If your incapacity began before you were 40 years old, you'll get £46.95; incapacity which began between 40 and 50 – £42.40; incapacity which began between 50 and 60 – £38.60; incapacity which began at 60 or older – £34.80. In addition, you may also be able to get extra payments for an adult dependant and your children – see **Appendix C – Extra Benefits for Dependants**.

How to claim and for more information. *Leaflet NI252 – Severe Disablement Allowance*, which you can get from your local DSS office, contains the necessary *claim form SDA1*.

If, however, you're not sufficiently ill to qualify for SDA, you may still be eligible for other benefits, such as the ones we look at next ...

DISABILITY LIVING ALLOWANCE

Disability Living Allowance (hereafter referred to as DLA) was introduced in April 1992 when it replaced and extended the help previously given by Mobility Allowance and Attendance Allowance to disabled people under the age of 65 – Attendance Allowance still remaining for those over that age.

DLA is a tax-free benefit for those under 65 who have personal care and/or mobility needs because of an illness or disability that has been present for a period of at least three months and is also likely to persist for a further six months. It is a non-contributory benefit which means that you do not need to have paid any National Insurance contributions to get it. Awards of DLA are determined by an Adjudication Officer who usually makes his decision on the basis of a claimant's own assessment of their needs.

The Allowance consists of two components:
1) The care component, which has three rates of help.
2) The mobility component, which has two rates.
Which rate you'll get of either or both components will depend on the amount of help you need with care and/or mobility.

Let us look at the mobility component (which is only payable to those aged 5 years or over) and see what counts as needing help to get around. You may qualify if you cannot walk at all; or were born without legs or feet; or had both legs amputated; or you have severe difficulties in walking; or because you are both deaf and blind; or you need help when you leave your home; or you have a severe mental impairment coupled with severe behavioural problems; or you're able to walk but you need someone with you when you're outdoors. Children over the age of 5 may qualify for help under this section but it must be clear that they need substantially more help than children of the same age who are not disabled.

You can also qualify for DLA because of your need for 'personal care'. Examples of what suitable needs might be, include: you need help with washing, dressing, using the toilet or other similar help; or you would need help if you tried to prepare a cooked main meal even if you had all the ingredients at hand (this provision only applies to claimants over the age of 16); or you need someone to keep an eye on you; or you need someone with you when you are on dialysis. Once again, the need has to be likely to continue for six months or more. There is no minimum age to qualify under this section and help may be available for both babies and children, but they must need substantially more help than other children of the same age and they must also have needed help for the past three months.

A very important point about DLA is that although the benefit is there to help you pay for care that you need, you don't necessarily have to be paying for the care or, for that matter, actually be receiving the care at all.

There is normally a three month waiting period before you can get DLA. But there are 'Special Rules' for people who suffer from a terminal illness and may not live longer than six months because of this. Under those special circumstances, there is no waiting period and the maximum amount of the personal care component of the benefit may be paid even if no help is needed. However, the mobility component will only be paid if the claimant actually needs help in getting around.

How much do you get? That depends upon whether you qualify for just one of the components or both. The 'care' component has three weekly rates: £45.70, £30.55 and £12.15; and the 'mobility' component has two rates: £31.95 and £12.15. Which rate you get will depend upon how your individual need is assessed. There is no means test for DLA and neither your income nor your savings will normally affect what you get. This benefit is usually completely ignored as income as far as claims for Income Support are concerned. And, you will also get the Christmas Bonus.

How to claim and for more information. You can get a claim pack by using the tear-off slip from *leaflet DSS704 – Disability Living Allowance*, which is available from the DSS or from Post Offices.

DLA is, of course, meant to help people with severe disabilities who would probably have great difficulty in working for a living. Nevertheless, should you be disabled and still be able to work you might well be entitled to collect as well the next benefit we look at.

DISABILITY WORKING ALLOWANCE

If you suffer from an illness or disability that limits your earning capacity, you may be entitled to receive Disability Working Allowance (hereafter referred to as DWA).

This is a benefit that is tax-free and which does not depend upon your National Insurance contributions record. However, this benefit is income-related and your savings will also affect how much you might get.

To qualify you have to meet the following conditions in the first instance:

a) You must be aged 16 or older.

b) Your illness or disability must limit your earning capacity.

c) You must be in receipt of Disability Living Allowance (see above) or have an invalid three-wheeler from the DSS; or for at least one of the 56 days before you claim you must have been receiving one of the following: Invalidity Benefit; Severe Disablement Allowance; or a disability premium as part of Income Support, Housing Benefit or Community Charge Benefit. You may also qualify under this section if you have been receiving Industrial Injuries Disablement Benefit (which includes constant attendance allowance); or a War Disablement Pension including constant attendance allowance or a mobility supplement; or Attendance Allowance.

d) You must be working at least 16 hours a week, but that can be either as an employee or as a self-employed person. If your job is a temporary one, you must expect it to last for at least five weeks.

e) You and your partner – if you have one – must not have savings totalling more than £16,000.

Additionally, you have to pass the Disability Test. This is usually done by signing a declaration that you meet the requirements and only rarely will a medical examination be needed. The DSS provides the following examples of reasons why you may qualify for DWA:

☐ Because of mental disability you need regular treatment for clinical depression, anxiety, phobias or other nervous or emotional problems; or your mental disability means that you often get confused; or you get so upset that you destroy things or hit people; or you always need someone to help you deal with money.

☐ During the last year you have suffered a fit or a coma during waking hours in which you lost consciousness.

☐ Exhaustion and/or pain stop you from working a normal working week because you have to keep stopping as a result of severe pain; or you become physically exhausted; or you get so tired that you can no longer concentrate on what you're doing.

☐ You are registered blind or partially sighted; or you cannot see to read a large print book.

☐ Your hearing is severely impaired; or you cannot make yourself understood; or you find it difficult to walk more than 100 metres without stopping or feeling severe pain; or the use of your hands is severely restricted.

Note that this is only a partial list and other conditions may well be acceptable. As with so many other benefits, the best advice is to put in a claim in any case.

How much do you get? The amount depends on whether you have a partner, how many children you have and their ages, how much money you have coming in – see **Appendix A – Common Rules** at the back of this book for more details. The current maximum weekly DWA benefit is £46.05 for a single adult and £63.75 for couples or lone parents. This payment is, of course, on top of whatever you might earn from your job and is tax-free. The benefit is awarded for 26 weeks at a time and generally remains the same during that period even if your circumstances change.

How to claim and for more information. Get *claim pack DWA1* from the DSS or a Post Office.

We will now look at other health-related benefits ...

ATTENDANCE ALLOWANCE

This is very similar to Disability Living Allowance (see above), except for the fact that it is a benefit for people disabled at or after the age of 65 who need a lot of care or supervision because of their illness or disablement.

This benefit – which is tax-free and does not depend upon your National Insurance contributions record – is paid regardless of savings or income and can be paid as well as other benefits, including Income Support. The conditions to qualify are broadly similar to those for Disability Living Allowance. However, you can normally only get Attendance Allowance if you have needed help with personal care for six months or more. But people who suffer from a terminal illness and are not expected to live longer than six months can claim straight away.

How much do you get? There are two weekly rates. The higher one of £45.70 is paid to people who need looking after day and night; the lower one of £30.55 is paid when attendance is only required by day or night.

How to claim and for more information. Get *leaflet DS702 – Attendance Allowance* from the DSS as it contains a reply-paid card that you can send off for a claim pack.

VACCINE DAMAGE PAYMENTS

If you were severely disabled as a result of vaccination you may be able to get a single tax-free payment.

To qualify, your disablement – which must be at least 80% – must be the result of having been vaccinated against one of the following diseases: diphtheria, tetanus, whooping cough, tuberculosis, poliomyelitis, measles, rubella (German measles) or mumps. A claim should also be made if you think you are severely disabled because you have been in close personal contact with a person who had been vaccinated against one of these diseases or because your mother was vaccinated while she was pregnant. The claim should be made within six years of the date following vaccination.

The vaccination must have taken place in the United Kingdom or the Isle of Man and generally it is also required that the vaccinated person was under the age of 18, but over the age of two. There are, however, some exceptions to that last condition.

How much do you get? A one-off payment of £30,000.

How to claim. You can get a claim form by writing to: *Vaccine Damage Payments Unit, Dept of Social Security, The Fylde Benefit and War Pensions Directorate, Norcross, Blackpool FY5 3TA.*

For more information. Get *leaflet HB3 – Payment for People Severely Disabled by a Vaccine.*

INDUSTRIAL INJURIES DISABLEMENT BENEFIT

This benefit may be available if you became disabled because of an accident at work or your disability was the result of one of the prescribed industrial diseases which include – among many others – the following examples: cramp or cellulitis of the hand, occupational deafness, anthrax, glanders, tuberculosis, viral hepatitis and different kinds of poisoning.

You don't have to be severely disabled to get benefit but you have to be at least 14% disabled. Most people receiving payment under this scheme are not severely disabled. Last year's payments totalled £600 million and went to some 300,000 beneficiaries.

What do you get? The highest weekly rate of Industrial Disablement Pension for claimants over the age of 18, or those under that age but with dependants, is £93.20 and this is for those who are 100% disabled; the lowest rate is £18.64 (20% disablement). Lower rates apply to claimants under 18 without dependants – ranging from £57.10 for 100% disablement to £11.42 for 20% disablement. There are also Allowances linked to the scheme. You may qualify for the **Reduced Earnings Allowance** (£37.28 maximum) if you can't return to your normal job because of the disability and your accident happened or your disease started before October 1st 1990. You may also qualify for **Constant Attendance Allowance** of £74.80 (maximum) if the relevant disability is 100% and you need constant care and attendance. Additionally, there is the **Exceptionally Severe Disablement Allowance** of £37.40 which may be payable if you are already entitled to Constant Attendance Allowance at one of the higher rates and the need for attendance is likely to be permanent.

How to claim. There are different claim forms for the various disabilities and *leaflet NI 6 – Industrial Injuries Disablement Benefit* tells you which one to use for your particular case.

For more information. See *leaflet NI 6* (mentioned above) and also the following: *NI 2 – If You Have an Industrial Disease*; *NI 207 – If You Think Your Job Has Made You Deaf*; *NI 237 – If You Have Asthma Because of Your Job*; and *NI 272 – If You Have* *a Disease Because of Working with Asbestos.* All of these are available from your local DSS office.

PNEUMOCONIOSIS, BYSSINOSIS AND MISCELLANEOUS DISEASES BENEFITS

These are special tax-free benefits for those who contracted pneumoconiosis, byssinosis and certain other connected diseases (all of them lung diseases caused by some dusts and fibres) as a result of employment before July 5th 1948. To qualify for the benefit you must not have been paid any compensation, industrial injuries benefits or damages for the disease.

Payments under this scheme are comparatively few and last year an average of 500 claimants were in receipt of this benefit at any given time at a total cost of £4 million.

How much do you get? This depends upon how disabled you are. The total weekly Disablement Allowance is £93.20 whereas the Partial Disablement Allowance currently stands at £34.50. You may also be able to get an 'unemployability supplement' of £57.60 and this may be further increased for early incapacity by one of three rates ranging from £12.15 to £3.80. There is also a **Constant Attendance Allowance** and an **Exceptionally Severe Disablement Allowance** with rates identical to those which apply to Industrial Disablement Benefit described above. There may also be extra payment for dependants. Additionally, if you are a dependant of someone who died as a result of these diseases, you may be able to claim a lump sum payment.

How to claim and for more information. If you contracted any of these diseases because of employment before July 5th 1948, use the *form PN 1A* that can be found in *leaflet PN1 – Pneumoconiosis, Byssinosis and Some Other Diseases from Work.* If you contracted the disease on or after July 5th 1948, you will need to get the appropriate claim form in the *BI 100* series. All of these are available from the DSS.

WORKMEN'S COMPENSATION SUPPLEMENT

If you were injured in an accident at work or contracted an industrial disease before July 5th 1948 and you are receiving Workmen's Compensation, you may also be entitled to this tax-free supplement, including possibly extra payments for dependants.

How to claim and for more information. Get *leaflet WS1 – Extra Cash with Workmen's Compensation* from your local DSS office.

The benefits listed above are all meant to help those who are either ill or have disabilities. There are also special benefits available for people who care for someone who has a disability or illness sufficiently severe to make daily life difficult. And, it doesn't matter whether the person you care for is young or old, is a relative or not, or whether you provide care occasionally or on a permanent basis.

Neither is it necessary that you should live with the person you care for and you may also share the caring with someone else. Even professional carers, who get paid for the job, may under certain circumstances still qualify for help.

It is worth noting that many people do not think of themselves as being 'carers' and therefore often miss out on the benefits to which they are entitled. In fact, it has been said that the Government's reliance on the good will of carers is such that millions of pounds remain unclaimed in this area alone.

There are two main benefits linked directly to caring ...

INVALID CARE ALLOWANCE

Expenditure on this benefit is estimated to be around £433 million in 1993/94 with around 251,000 carers receiving benefit at any one time.

You may be eligible to get Invalid Care Allowance (hereafter referred to as ICA) if you and the person you care for meet the following requirements.

a) The person being cared for is in receipt of Disability Living Allowance or Attendance Allowance or Constant Attendance Allowance (in the latter instance under the Industrial Injuries or War Pensions schemes).

b) You're between the ages of 16 and 65.

c) At least 35 hours of your time are devoted to your caring duties.

d) You earn no more than £50 a week after deducting reasonable expenses.

How much do you get? The current basic rate of ICA is £34.50 a week. This basic rate may, however, be increased according to your circumstances, especially if you yourself have to support people, such as children, a husband or wife or even another adult who looks after your children. The extra you may be able to claim will be governed by the other person's circumstances.

ICA is, however, taxable and you should declare it on your annual Income Tax Return. On the other hand, the Christmas Bonus which you may also get as part of your ICA entitlement is free of tax.

Why you might not get ICA. There are two main reasons why ICA might not be granted:

a) If you're in full-time education, which in this context means 21 or more hours of supervised study a week, or on holiday from full-time education.

b) If you're working and earn more than £50 a week, after deducting from your take-home pay the costs of going to work, such as fares, petrol, lunches and payments to child-minders. If you are in doubt as to whether you are earning too much to qualify for ICA, apply anyway as the DSS's calculation might be different from yours and you might well qualify after all.

How to claim and for more information. Get *claim pack DS700 – Invalid Care Allowance* which is available from the DSS or Post Offices.

HOME RESPONSIBILITIES PROTECTION

This is a scheme designed to protect the State Pension rights of people who are not working because they are looking after someone else, be it a child or a sick or disabled person. Home Responsibilities Protection (hereafter referred to as HRP) is, of course, given to people bringing up children but it is also available for carers.

Who qualifies for HRP? There are two main qualifications that you must meet to get HRP as a carer for someone other than a child:

a) Your caring duties must take up at least 35 hours a week and 48 weeks in the year.

b) The person you care for must be getting either Attendance Allowance or Constant Attendance Allowance paid with Industrial Injuries, War or Service Pensions; or the highest or middle rate of the care component of Disability Living Allowance; or you must be receiving Income Support to look after the person you're caring for.

You can also get HRP if you're getting Income Support without having to be available for work because you're looking after a sick or disabled child or adult at home.

If you are receiving Income Support to look after the person, you should have received HRP automatically and there should be no need to apply, but it's just as well to check that this was done.

On the other hand, you do need to apply if the person cared for is in receipt of either Attendance Allowance or Constant Attendance Allowance.

What do you get? You receive free National Insurance credits, the same as if you were paying the weekly contribution. This, in turn, will affect your possible entitlement to contributory benefits and will serve to protect your State Retirement Pension. Although the benefit of receiving HRP may not be obvious now, it will be relevant when you reach pensionable age.

How to claim and for more information. Get *form CF411* from your DSS office.

SPECIAL NOTE

As has been mentioned earlier, major changes in both Sickness Benefit (see previous chapter) and Invalidity Benefit (at the beginning of this chapter) are likely to take place from April 1995. However, the Bill – The Social Security (Incapacity for Work) Bill 1994 – that will implement these changes is currently before Parliament and as such is subject to amendment.

The main points of the proposed changes are:

□ Sickness Benefit and Invalidity Benefit will be replaced with a single new benefit, Incapacity Benefit (IB), from April 1995.

□ Incapacity Benefit will consist of two elements: short-term and long-term IB. Short-term IB will be payable for the first 52 weeks of incapacity. For the first 28 weeks, the rate will be set at the current Sickness Benefit rate. For weeks 29 to 52, an amount equivalent to the higher rate of Statutory Sick Pay will be payable. Long-term IB will be payable, after 52 weeks of incapacity for work, at an amount equivalent to the basic rate of Invalidity Benefit and will not be payable after pension age. The two highest rates of IB will be taxable.

□ Two rates of 'age addition' will be paid with long-term IB based on the claimant's age when incapacity started. No earnings-related additional pension will be payable. There will also be changes in the entitlement conditions for adult dependency increases. Transitional arrangements will be made for existing Sickness Benefit and Invalidity Benefit recipients when the new benefit is introduced.

□ The Government also plans to introduce with IB a new medical test – which they describe as 'more objective' – of incapacity for work. The new test will apply after 28 weeks of incapacity for work and will assess ability to perform a range of work-related activities rather than the ability to perform a specific job. Non-medical factors such as education, skills and experience will not be taken into account.

7 How To Collect Free Prescriptions And Other Health Benefits

Help is available to cover the costs of National Health Service items for a wide variety of people. Generally, you can get whatever it is free for one of two reasons: either because you're part of a group that has an automatic entitlement; or because your income and savings are below a certain level.

We will now look at the various priced NHS items one by one, each time listing those groups automatically entitled to get them free. For convenience's sake, the details of how to qualify and claim on the basis of low income are covered at the end of this chapter where you will also find out how to get more information.

NATIONAL HEALTH SERVICE PRESCRIPTIONS

The current prescription charge is £4.75 per item, but you can get free prescriptions if you are in one of the groups of people shown below. Everyone who is entitled to free prescriptions must complete and sign the declaration on the back of the prescription form before handing it to the pharmacist, but some people must also first get an exemption certificate, or a certificate of full remission from the NHS Low Income Scheme.

You need only complete and sign the back of the prescription form to get free prescriptions if you are:

☐ A woman aged 60 or older; a man aged 65 or older; a child under the age of 16 years; a young person aged 16 or older, but under 19, who is in full-time education; someone receiving Income Support or Family Credit; the partner of someone receiving Income Support or Family Credit.

You need an exemption certificate to get free prescriptions if you are:

☐ An expectant mother.
☐ A mother who has had a baby in the last 12 months.
☐ Someone with one of the specified medical conditions listed in *leaflet P11*. Included amongst these conditions are: a permanent fistula which requires continuous surgical dressing or an appliance; epilepsy requiring continuous anti-convulsive

therapy; a continuing physical disability which stops you from going outdoors unless with the help of someone else; diabetes mellitus (except where treatment is by diet alone); myxoedema or other similar conditions where supplemental thyroid hormone is necessary; hypoparathyroidism; diabetes insipidus or other forms of hypopituitarism; various forms of hypoadrenalism (including Addison's disease) when specific substitution therapy is essential; and myasthenia gravis. It's also important to note that temporary disabilities do not count, even though their effect may be long lasting.

□ Someone who is a war or MoD disablement pensioner – in this instance, however, only the prescriptions you get for your accepted disability are free.

War or MoD disablement pensioners are automatically issued with an exemption certificate when their pensions are awarded. Other people need to get an exemption certificate from their local Family Health Services Authority – hereafter referred to as FHSA – or Health Board in Scotland. You'll find the address of your local FHSA or Health Board in your phone book. To get an exemption certificate you will need to fill in a claim form:

□ Expectant mothers must fill in *form FW8*, given to them by their doctor, midwife or health visitor, and send it to the FHSA.

□ Mothers who have had a baby in the last 12 months must complete *form A* in *leaflet P11* and send it to the FHSA.

□ People who suffer from one of the medical conditions listed in *leaflet P11* must complete *form B* in the leaflet, ask their doctor to sign it, and then send it to the FHSA.

If you are not in one of the groups of people already mentioned, but are over 16, on a low income, and your capital is £8,000 or less, you may be entitled to free prescriptions under the NHS Low Income Scheme. To do this you will have to get a certificate of full charge remission from the Health Benefits Division of the Prescription Pricing Authority. You apply for this by completing *form AG1*, which you can get from local Benefits Agency offices, FHSAs, doctors, dentists, opticians and NHS hospitals, and sending it to: *The Health Benefits Division, Sandyford House, Newcastle-upon-Tyne NE2 1DB*.

If you don't qualify for free prescriptions, you may still be able to save some money by buying a so-called 'season ticket', a prescription prepayment certificate. These certificates are available for either four months or one year at a cost of £24.60 or £67.70

respectively. These certificates will save you money if you need more than five items on prescription in a four-month period or more than 14 items in a year.

To buy a prescription prepayment certificate you must complete *form FP95* (*EC95* in Scotland). You can get the form from your FHSA, Post Offices or chemists, and after completing it you should send it to your local FHSA together with your payment.

NHS DENTAL TREATMENT

Certain dental treatments are available free of charge to everyone, and these include: repairs to dentures; stopping bleeding; calling a dentist out to his surgery in an emergency; and home visits if necessary. However, do note that while there is no extra charge for seeing a dentist out of hours for an emergency or at home, you will have to pay for any treatment in the usual way unless you're entitled to free treatment.

You will automatically be entitled to get free dental treatment if: you're under 18; or you're under 19 but still in full-time education; or you're receiving either Income Support or Family Credit or are the partner of someone receiving either of those two benefits; or you or your partner hold a valid NHS Low Income Scheme certificate AG2; or you're expecting a baby and were pregnant when the dentist accepted you for treatment; or you've had a baby during the 12 months before your dental treatment began.

How to claim. Tell your dentist that you're entitled to free treatment.

Certain War Pensioners may be able to get a refund of statutory NHS charges for dental examination or treatment or dentures if these were needed because of a disability for which they receive a War Pension. They should claim by sending the receipt from the dentist to: *War Pensions Branch, DSS, North Fylde Central Office, Norcross, Blackpool FY5 3TA.*

NHS SIGHT TESTS AND VOUCHERS FOR GLASSES

SIGHT TESTS

Since April 1st 1989, free NHS sight tests are now only available to certain groups of people. You are entitled if you: are under 16, or aged 16 or over but under 19 and still in full-time education; or are receiving either Income Support or Family Credit; are the partner of someone receiving either of those benefits; or you or your partner have a valid NHS Low Income Scheme certificate AG2; or are registered blind or partially sighted; or are a diagnosed diabetic or glaucoma patient; or are aged 40 or older and are the parent, brother, sister or child of a diagnosed glaucoma patient; or are a patient of the Hospital Eye Service and have been advised by your doctor or consultant to seek a sight test from your optician. You claim your free sight test simply by completing a form at your opticians. The information you provide may, however, be checked later.

Additionally, you qualify for a free sight test if you have to wear complex lenses. To claim you need to show the person who tests your sight a copy of your prescription for glasses or the optician may be able to check your prescription by examining your current glasses.

NHS VOUCHERS FOR HELP WITH OPTICAL COSTS

This is a scheme that helps with the costs of glasses or contact lenses by providing a voucher than can be used towards their purchase. If your glasses cost more than any voucher you're given, you'll have to pay the difference yourself.

You are automatically entitled to an NHS glasses voucher if you: are under 16; or are aged 16 or over but under 19 and still in full-time education; or you are receiving either Income Support or Family Credit; or are the partner of someone who is getting either of these benefits; or you or your partner hold a valid NHS Low Income Scheme certificate AG2. You claim your voucher by ticking the voucher entitlement box when you sign the sight test form.

You are also entitled to a voucher if you're prescribed glasses with at least one exceptionally powerful lens – your optician will tell you if this applies to you.

Some War Pensioners may also be entitled to claim back some or all of the costs of their sight test and glasses if these are needed because of the disability for which they get a War Pension. Claim by writing to: *Treatment Group, War Pensions Directorate, DSS, Norcross, Blackpool FY5 3TA*, including with your claim your sight test receipt and any vouchers.

There is one more group that may be entitled and these are Hospital Eye Service patients who need frequent changes of glasses or contact lenses. You'll be given a special voucher if your consultant decides that you're entitled for clinical reasons.

How much your voucher is worth towards the cost of your glasses varies considerably. First of all, after your sight test, the optician marks your voucher with a letter code that decides the maximum amount of help the voucher can give you towards the cost of your new glasses. But you won't necessarily get the full value of the voucher unless you're in the automatic entitlement group shown above.

Full details of how the voucher scheme works out in practice can be found in *leaflet G11 – NHS Sight Tests and Vouchers for Glasses* which you can get from Benefits Agency offices, your family doctor or optician.

NHS HOSPITAL TRAVEL COSTS

You can get help with the cost of travel to and from hospital for NHS treatment and have automatic entitlement to this if you: get either Income Support or Family Credit; or are the partner or dependant child of someone who is getting either of these benefits; or are the patient of a sexually transmitted disease clinic which is more than 15 miles from your home; or are getting a War or MoD Disablement Pension and are being treated in an NHS hospital for your disability. Other patients who are assessed as being on low income and whose savings do not exceed £8,000 are entitled to a full or partial refund of hospital travel costs.

The travel costs that normally can be paid include: public transport fares; estimated amount of petrol used if you travel by private car; a contribution towards costs if you travel to hospital by a local voluntary car scheme; and taxi fares – but these will only be paid if there is no other way you can travel for all or part of the journey.

There are special arrangements for people living in the area covered by the Highlands and Islands Development Board who have to travel at least 30 miles (or more than five miles by water) and those living in the Isles of Scilly who have to come to the mainland for hospital treatment.

There are several different ways to claim these costs and full details will be found in DSS *leaflet H11 – NHS Hospital Travel Costs*.

NHS WIGS AND FABRIC SUPPORTS

You're automatically entitled to get free wigs and fabric supports if you: are a hospital in-patient when the item is supplied; or are under 16; or are 16 and over but under 19 and still in full-time education; are getting either Family Credit or Income Support; or are the partner of someone who is receiving either of these benefits; or you're a War Pensioner and the wig or support is needed because of your war disability.

The claiming procedure for once is fairly easy: when you go to the hospital to have your wig or support fitted, tell them that you're automatically entitled to have the item supplied free.

You'll find full details of this scheme in DSS *leaflet WF11 – NHS Wigs and Fabric Supports*.

FREE MILK AND VITAMINS

If you belong to one of the groups listed below, you're entitled to help with obtaining milk and vitamins.

☐ If you're getting Income Support you may be entitled to liquid milk or dried milk. Milk – if someone in your family is pregnant or you have a child under five years old you are entitled to seven pints or eight half litres of milk a week for each child or pregnant woman. A breast-feeding mother can drink the milk herself. Dried baby milk – if you are bottle-feeding one or more babies under one year old, you are entitled to receive 900 grammes of dried baby milk a week for each child. This is instead of liquid milk. If you become pregnant, tell the DSS the date the baby is due. They will give you tokens for seven pints or eight half litres of milk a week for yourself until the baby is born. Additionally, if you're a mother or an expectant mother you can get free vitamins while you are pregnant or breast-feeding, and for your children under the age of five years. You obtain the vitamins at a maternity or child health clinic.

☐ If you're getting Family Credit, you don't get free milk but the rate of Family Credit for children under the age of five years is increased to compensate for this. However, you can get dried milk for under fives at specially reduced prices at maternity and child health clinics.

☐ If your child is disabled, you can get tokens which can be exchanged for seven pints of milk a week. To qualify the disabled child must be between the ages of five and 16 years and not be registered at school because of disablement. To claim, complete *form FW10*, available from your local Benefits Agency office, or write to: *Room A110A, Warbreck House, Warbreck Hill Road, Blackpool FY2 OUZ.*

Additionally, it's worth noting that some clinics sell vitamins and dried baby milk at special low prices to people not in receipt of Income Support or Family Credit.

LOW INCOME ENTITLEMENT TO HEALTH BENEFITS

You may also be entitled to help with the cost of NHS services listed in this chapter (except milk and vitamins) on the grounds of low income, but that help won't be available if your capital exceeds £8,000. You may qualify for help if your capital is £8,000 or less and the money you have left each week is less than set amounts that take into consideration your family circumstances.

The calculation follows those used to determine Income Support and works by comparing your weekly resources and requirements. Your requirements will be the same as the Income Support allowances and premiums for specific needs, plus your housing costs and Council Tax, after taking off any Housing Benefit and Council Tax Benefit that you get.

How to claim: You claim on *form AG1* which you can get from Benefits Agency offices, hospitals, doctors, opticians and dentists. Send your completed form in the envelope provided to: *Health Benefits Division, Prescription Pricing Authority, Sandyford House, Newcastle-upon-Tyne NE2 1DB.* Your claim will be assessed and if you qualify you will be sent a certificate that lasts six months and covers both you and your dependants. There is, however, no need to claim if you already have automatic entitlement or alternatively already have a valid certificate. Incidentally, it's worth adding that if you're aged 16 or more you are entitled to claim in your own right even if you are still living with your parents.

How much help do you get? This depends upon what kind of certificate you get.

☐ If your requirements are more than your resources, you will be sent certificate AG2 which entitles you to the maximum help available.

☐ If your resources are more than your requirements, you will instead be sent certificate AG3 for limited help. This means that you're not entitled to help with the cost of prescriptions, but will get help with travel costs to the extent that they are more than your excess weekly income. You will also have to pay three times your excess weekly income (the so-called assessed contribution) towards the cost of NHS dental treatment or a wig or fabric support, or the actual cost if this is less. If you need optical treatment, you will first pay for your sight test and if there is any of your assessed contribution left after that, this amount will be used to reduce the value of your optical voucher.

For more information. See Department of Health *leaflet AB11 Help with NHS Costs* which is available from Benefits Agency offices, Post Offices and family doctors. There are also other leaflets about specific services: *D11 – NHS Dental Treatment*; *G11 – NHS Sight Tests and Vouchers for Glasses*; *H11 – NHS Prescriptions*; *WF11 – NHS Wigs and Fabric Supports*. These are all available from Benefits Agency offices and family doctors. Some of them may also be obtainable from dentists, opticians, pharmacists or hospitals.

8 How To Collect Unemployment Benefit

The provision of benefits linked to unemployment continues to remain one of the major drains upon the resources of the social security system. While there can be some argument about how accurately the Government figures represent the true number of those out of work, there is little doubt that for the immediately foreseeable future those figures will continue to remain high. However, after many years during which the unemployment level rose steadily, it is encouraging to note that in February 1994, the official number of jobless stood at 2.75 million, a figure significantly less than that of a year before.

Critics say that the real figure is much higher, particularly so far as young people and married women are concerned. It is not part of the brief of this book to get involved in a political debate, but it can be safely assumed that many who could genuinely register as unemployed haven't done so because it would provide very little, if any, benefit for them. Despite that, there are substantial benefits available for the unemployed and we shall look at these in detail in just a moment.

In the meantime, however, a few brief statistics to give an overview of the size of the problem. During the year 1992 to 1993, unemployed people received over £9,000 million in Social Security Benefits. The Employment Service, an agency within the Employment Department Group, which itself employs some 48,000 people, runs 1,200 Jobcentres and Unemployment Benefit Offices, these currently being in the process of becoming integrated to provide all aspects of the service under one roof in each locality.

So, what does this mammoth organisation provide for the jobless? Well, quite a few things. One of the most obvious ones, of course, is the Unemployment Benefit, which we will look at first.

UNEMPLOYMENT BENEFIT

Major changes in the administration of this benefit are likely to take place in the near future as it has been proposed that it will be replaced by a 'Job Searcher's Allowance' in 1995 and that this will eventually be paid for six months only. In the meantime, Unemployment Benefit continues much as it has been in previous years.

Known as the 'dole' in the bad old days, Unemployment Benefit (hereafter referred to as UB) is a weekly payment to partially replace lost wages or salaries.

Currently, you're usually entitled to receive this benefit if you:

a) Are capable of, and available for, work on every day for which you make a claim.

b) Are actively seeking employment in every week in which you make a claim.

c) Have paid or have been credited with enough of the right kind of National Insurance contributions.

Let us now look at these conditions in detail.

Capable of and available for work. The capable bit refers to being physically capable of doing the kind of work you are looking for and this clause would disqualify you if you were sick during your jobless spell. The 'available' condition can be a bit trickier as by this the DSS normally means that you should be able to 'start work immediately', although there are some exceptions to this as, for example, you may once a year go for up to a fortnight to a work camp organised by a charity or local authority. You would also probably be regarded as available if you were a member of an organised group responding to an emergency, for example a volunteer fireman or lifeboatman.

You would also be treated as being available if you were caring for a child or a sick or elderly person – providing, that is, you were able and willing to give up this activity at 24 hours' notice. Additionally, someone involved in doing voluntary work may be allowed 48 hours' notice in which to make arrangements to give up or rearrange their voluntary responsibilities.

Actively seeking employment. It means that you must be able to show that each week you have taken reasonable steps to find a job. How this is interpreted varies somewhat because you can hardly apply for jobs that don't exist. Nevertheless, you may be asked to prove that you're trying your best. Somewhat linked to this condition is the fact that you musn't 'unreasonably restrict' your chances of getting a job by being unrealistic about what you'll consider. Says the DSS: "If you put restrictions on the kind of work you're seeking, the hours you can work, the pay you want, where you will work, you must show that – despite these restrictions – you have a reasonable chance of getting a job. Otherwise, you will not get Unemployment Benefit." Despite that, you will get UB if you can prove that your restrictions are reasonable. And, in this context 'reasonable' can mean that the existence of temporary industrial conditions in your area makes it impossible for you to get the kind of work you want; or that the restrictions arise from your physical or mental condition; or "the restrictions are related to and are consistent with the conditions of your usual occupation". However, this last restriction will only be accepted for a limited length of time and never for more than 13 weeks.

National Insurance contributions. To qualify under this section, you usually have to meet two conditions in the "two relevant tax years", these being the last two complete tax years before the start of your benefit year. These conditions are: 1) You must have paid Class 1 contributions on earnings of at least 25 times the lower earnings limit in one of these two years (credits do not count for this condition); and 2) You must have paid or been credited with Class 1 contributions on earnings of at least 50 times the lower earnings limit in both of the two relevant tax years.

So, if you meet all of these conditions, you should receive UB – after you sign on, of course.

How to claim. You apply for UB by signing on at your local Unemployment Benefit Office (UBO) or Jobcentre – some areas still have both, others have Jobcentres that combine the two roles. You can find the address by looking in your telephone directory under 'Employment, Department of'.

Whatever you do, don't delay in getting your claim in because they usually can't be backdated. If you can't get to the Jobcentre (or UBO) on your very first day of unemployment, phone them to register your intention of making a claim.

When you go along to the office, you will initially be interviewed by a 'New Client Adviser' who will give you advice about job hunting and training as well as register your claim.

How much do you get? There is a single flat rate of £45.45 a week for men and women under state pension age. If you're over state pension age this goes up to £57.60. You will also be able to claim extra for an adult dependant who looks after your children: £28.05 (if you're under state pension age) or £34.50 (over state pension age). Benefit is payable for up to a year and taxable, but it is not affected by your savings or your partner's earnings.

Your benefit may, however, be less than that. If you're 55 or older and receive more than £35 a week (gross) from an occupational or personal pension scheme, your UB will be reduced by 10p for every 10p that your pension exceeds £35.

There is also an age limitation on UB as men can't get it after age 70 and women after age 65.

QUESTIONS AND ANSWERS ON UNEMPLOYMENT BENEFIT

Q: Do I have to sign on every week at the Jobcentre or UBO?

A: No, the arrangements vary, although you will be asked to visit the office regularly to maintain your claim. Special arrangements can often be made for people who live a long way away or if it would be very difficult for you to get there.

Q: How is the benefit paid?

A: You will usually be paid by Girocheque. Normally this is posted on the day after you sign to claim, so it will usually arrive by the third working day after you sign. Benefit is normally claimed and paid in arrears every two weeks.

Q: What happens when my UB runs out?

A: Having received your maximum amount of UB, you cannot get it again until you re-qualify by working as an employee for at least 16 hours a week for 13 weeks. However, when UB expires, you are entitled to claim for Income Support

Q: I quit my last job – can I still get UB?

A: That depends on the reason why you quit as normally you will not be entitled to UB for a period of up to 26 weeks if you left your job voluntarily without good cause. What is 'good cause' can vary tremendously according to the circumstances and it will be up to you to show that you had good reason to quit. If your reason is accepted, you'll get UB.

Q: Can you get UB if you're fired?

A: Yes, but you will not get it for the first 26 weeks if you lost your job through 'misconduct', which can mean simply that you did something or failed to do something which would make a reasonable employer consider you no longer fit to hold your job. But it is not enough for your employer simply to say that you were dismissed·for misconduct, so both you and your employer will be asked by the DSS to say why your job came to an end.

Q: Can I get UB while I am out on strike?

A: The answer to this is 'no'. But you may be able to claim UB during a stoppage if you haven't withdrawn your labour and have no direct interest in the outcome of the dispute.

Q: I've been made redundant and actually received a rather large payment. Will that affect my UB?

A: No, it shouldn't. Other payments that usually do not stop you from claiming UB are: wages due, holiday pay, payments from the employment – whether in money or in kind – which arose before the job ended and refunded occupational pension scheme contributions. However, you should tell the Jobcentre about any payments you received, even if this will be ignored by them.

For more information. See DSS *leaflet FB9 – Unemployed?* or *NI12 – Unemployment Benefit.* There are also a number of interesting leaflets and booklets available free of charge at your Jobcentre which may help you, including *Redundancy Payments, Redundancy Consultation and Notification, Unfairly Dismissed? Fact Sheet on Employment Law: Notice and Reasons for Dismissal.*

HELP IN FINDING A JOB

Apart from registering claims for benefit, the Jobcentres can also help you find a job. Although – with one exception – these are not cash benefits they may still be very valuable to you.

Here's what is on offer:

VACANCIES REGISTER

Various job vacancies are displayed on cards and you pick what might suit you and ask about them at the desk where you will be given more information about each job. If the job still seems suitable, interviews will be arranged for you. What you might actually find on display will vary considerably from area to area. But, says the Department of Employment: "New jobs come in every day so it's a good idea to call in often or keep in touch by phone."

THIRTEEN-WEEK JOB REVIEW

After you've been out of work for about three months, you'll be asked to go in to the Jobcentre where you'll see a Client Adviser who is described as 'an expert in the local job market'. They will advise on various ways to make your search for employment more successful and review your back-to-work plan.

JOB SEARCH SEMINARS

You may wish to attend one of these if you've been out of work for more than three months as they offer 'two days of expert help on the best ways to search out and apply for jobs.' Your fares to attend the seminar will be reimbursed.

JOB REVIEW WORKSHOP

There are two-day workshops designed to help you assess what you have to offer and perhaps lead you to consider changing direction and look at alternative jobs. These workshops are available to those who have been unemployed for three months or longer and, once again, your fares to attend will be paid.

JOBCLUB

Aimed at those who have been out of work for more than six months – although this rule is relaxed for disabled people and ex-offenders – Jobclubs are described as "a better approach to help you get a job". Says the literature: "We hear of lots of jobs that never get advertised. We show you ways to perform well on the telephone and at interviews, and how to write a more effective job application."

One big advantage of the Jobclub scheme is that you can use their stamps, telephones, newspapers, stationery and other resources free of charge. And, once again, your fares to attend are paid.

JOB INTERVIEW GUARANTEE (JIG)

Again, this scheme is primarily meant for those who have been out of work for more than six months, although it may be available under special circumstances to those who have been jobless for less than that time. It offers, among other things, a place on a one-week pre-recruitment course designed to help you succeed at an interview with a local employer. And the DoE stress that "you'll be guaranteed an interview for a job at the end". Originally, the JIG scheme only operated in certain selected areas, but it is now available nationally.

RESTART AND RESTART COURSE

A major feature linked to these schemes is a five-day course which will give you a chance to rethink and plan your future and consider alternative employment, including the possibilities of becoming self-employed.

TRAVEL TO INTERVIEW SCHEME

This scheme will pay for your travel costs and unavoidable overnight stays to go to a job interview. To qualify for this you must have been out of a job for at least four weeks and the interview must be: a) with an employer who has confirmed it; and b) beyond normal daily travelling distance from your home; and c) in the United Kingdom. The job must also be for at least 30 hours a week and be expected to last more than a year. You will not be able to claim, however, if the job is expected to attract earnings above a set limit – currently this is £25,000 a year.

Full details of the scheme and how to apply are available from all Jobcentres and it is important that you should apply before you travel.

COMMUNITY ACTION

This is a voluntary scheme available for those who have been unemployed and receiving benefits for a year or longer. Its purpose is to give people the opportunity to gain experience on projects that will benefit the community and at the same time provide them with practical help in their search for work. Projects under the Community Action umbrella cover a wide range of areas, including environmental and recycling initiatives, caring, as well as administrative or research projects. When the programme was launched in September 1993, it was announced that it would provide a total of 60,000 opportunities during a full year, with up to 20,000 participants being involved at any one time. In practice, participants in the scheme will be provided with part-time work opportunities and, in addition, will also be given individually structured jobsearch assistance and access to resources such as newspapers and telephones to help them get back to work. Participants will also receive a reference covering their time spent in Community Action, this being initially limited to a maximum of six months. Each participant will receive an allowance from the Employment Service equivalent to their benefit and topped up by an extra £10 a week. If appropriate, a contribution towards travel costs will also be paid. Ask at your Jobcentre about Community Action projects available in your area.

WORK TRIAL

Launched in April of 1993, this scheme, which is described as "providing an opportunity to try out an actual job and show an employer what you can do", has only in recent months been promoted heavily by Jobcentres in their advertisements. The principle behind the scheme is simple: the 'work trial' is entirely voluntary: you don't lose any benefit while you're doing it and hopefully you will be offered a job at the end of it. Early results have, however, so far proven somewhat disappointing in that four out of ten who took part in Work Trial failed to get jobs at the end of it. Despite that, it is expected that the scheme will be extended and that some 15,000 people will participate in it during the next 12 months. While you're on Work Trial you won't get anything from your employer, but will receive travelling expenses (up to £5 a day) and meal expenses (up to £1.50 daily), these being paid either by the employer or your Jobcentre without your benefit being affected. For more details, see the Work Trial Specialist at your Jobcentre.

For more information. These are just some of the leaflets and booklets available free of charge from your Jobcentre – *Just the Job, Make It Work, Jobseeker's Charter, How to be Better Off in Work,* and *Jobhunting (a Guide for Managers, Executives and Professionals).*

Your Jobcentre can also offer free help with all kinds of training and retraining. We look at these schemes in more detail in the next chapter.

9 How To Get Free Job Training And Interest-Free Careers Loans

The first part of this chapter is devoted to the free job training opportunities provided by the Government and later on you're shown how you can collect an interest-free loan to learn almost any skill.

Most job training is provided under the auspices of local Training and Enterprise Councils – in Scotland, they are known as Local Enterprise Companies. These Councils, generally referred to as TECs, are funded from Government sources and contract with other organisations to provide the training opportunities.

You contact them via your local Jobcentre or Careers Office where you will be given details of what your local TEC has available. Although what is on offer can vary considerably from area to area, there are national guidelines for several different programmes.

YOUTH TRAINING

This is supposed to be available to all 16 and 17 year olds not in school. Says the literature: "If you are 16 or 17 and are not in a job or full-time education, you are guaranteed the offer of a suitable place." The same guarantee also applies to those aged 18 or over who had not been able to take up a place earlier because of disability, ill health, pregnancy, language difficulties and certain other reasons.

The training offered can cover almost all types of occupation and is given either by specialist training firms, employers, colleges, local authorities or voluntary bodies. Check with your local Jobcentre for what is available in your locality.

How much do you get? Apart from the training which is, of course, free of charge, you'll be paid a training allowance. This is at least £29.50 a week for those aged 16. If you are 17 or over you will get at least £35 a week and in some circumstances may also get help with travel, lodging and other support costs.

There are also schemes in some areas where you can be given a training credit to buy your own training.

TRAINING FOR WORK

Available to those who have been out of work for six months or longer, Training for Work is designed to help unemployed adults to train or gain useful work experience. According to the Department of Employment, this scheme "offers a range of opportunities to train or gain work experience that is directly related to the job you want to do". Exactly what is available under this scheme varies widely from area to area and you will have to check with your own Jobcentre to find out what's on offer. Generally, participants will be given help with travel expenses, child care costs and other costs associated with the training programme.

LEARNING FOR WORK

One of the new measures to help unemployed people announced in the 1993 Budget, Learning for Work is a scheme that is described as providing "your opportunity to follow a full-time course leading to a vocationally relevant qualification". Course fees will be paid on your behalf and you will receive an allowance equivalent to your benefit for up to a year. Once again, check with your Jobcentre to find out what's available near you.

OPEN LEARNING

Open Learning is defined as "learning built around you – you learn at your own pace, and at a time and place to suit you. Whether you want to learn to operate a computer, learn management skills or bricklaying, there is likely to be an open learning package to suit you." These packages may include text books, audio and video material and may also be supported by practical sessions.

You can find out more about Open Learning at your local Jobcentre where there will be a copy of the Open Learning Directory which lists more than 2,000 opportunities and the addresses of your local centres. The financial arrangements vary and you can get help through the Career Development Loan scheme – see further on.

Your Jobcentre will also offer what is known as 'Business and Enterprise Services for the Unemployed'. You'll find full details of this in the next chapter.

CAREER DEVELOPMENT LOANS

This is a scheme that was launched in 1988 and provides interest-free loans for eligible people to help them pay for vocational training. To date, nearly 50,000 people have received loans totalling more than £125 million and in the last financial year (1993-94) some 12,000 loans were made. The Employment Department is planning to extend the scheme further and its current target is to make 20,000 loans during 1994/95.

To qualify for one of these loans – known as CDLs – you must be able to say 'yes' to the following four conditions:

a) You are aged 18 or over and will not be receiving a mandatory grant, full discretionary award or other financial support for the costs you need a CDL to cover.

b) The course you intend to take must last between one week and one year and is suitable for the work you want to do in the UK or elsewhere in the EC after you complete your training.

c) If you're employed, your employer is not contributing to the fees, receiving a grant or paying your wages if the course is full-time.

d) You will be applying for a loan of not less than £200 and not more than £5,000 and would not otherwise have funds to pay for the training.

CDLs are available through a partnership arrangement between the Employment Department and three High Street banks – Barclays, the Co-operative and the Clydesdale. You apply to one of these to borrow the money you need to train – within the limits specified above – and to cover up to 80% of course fees, plus the full cost of books, materials and other course expenses. You may also be able to borrow money for living expenses if your course is full-time.

You won't have to make any repayments while you are training and for up to one month afterwards and during this time the interest on the loan is paid for you.

How much do you get? Essentially what it amounts to is that the Government will pay the interest on your loan while you're training. You, of course, remain responsible for repaying the loan itself. So, how much you actually benefit depends on how much you borrow and for how long.

How to apply. Either by phoning 0800 585 505 free of charge between 9am and 9pm; or asking for an information booklet by writing to *Career Development Loans, FREEPOST, Newcastle-upon-Tyne X NE85 1BR*; or by enquiring at your local Jobcentre or TEC.

QUESTIONS AND ANSWERS ON CDLs

Q: Are there restrictions on what kind of courses qualify for CDLs?

A: No, not really, apart from the fact that the course must be vocational, that is related to the job you want to do. And, courses can be full-time, part-time, open or distance learning.

Q: Does taking a CDL-assisted course affect my Unemployment Benefit?

A: Yes, it will if your course stops you from being available for work. If you are receiving either Unemployment Benefit or Income Support, you should check with your local office before applying for a CDL.

Q: What kind of people have taken out CDLs in the past?

A: The following two examples were provided by the Employment Department: Giovanna Battiston, a university student took out a loan because she realised that she needed a further qualification to improve her employment prospects. She chose a Master of Philosophy course in publishing studies at Swansea University. Now aged 23, Giovanna works for the publishing department of Thomas Cook as an editorial assistant and is sure that the course funded by her CDL helped her get the job.

Another case is that of Fiona Sommerville from Aberdeen who had had a varied nursing career and completed a wide range of professional courses, which included firefighting and survival. Fiona used her CDL to complete a four-week HSE Offshore Medic training course and she is now the medic on a support vessel responsible for about 300 personnel on an oil rig platform in the North Sea.

Q: What if the course I take doesn't help me find a job? Am I still responsible for paying off the loan?

A: Yes, you certainly are and you should consider this very carefully beforehand. It is stressed in the application form that neither the bank making the loan nor ·the Employment Department accept responsibility for any inadequacy or unsuitability of the training you receive. If you should be dissatisfied with the training you have received, you will have to deal with the training provider directly.

Q: Where can I find out about suitable courses?

A: Obvious places to enquire are your local advice centre, Employment Service office, TEC or library as well as universities, colleges, etc. There is also a service known as TAP – which stands for 'training access points' – which is a user-friendly database of training and education opportunities in your area and which may also include open learning information. There may be a TAP in your local library or Jobcentre.

10 How To Collect Grants And Loans To Start Your Own Business

In recent years greater emphasis has been put by Government on ways to help people become self-employed as a way of countering the rising numbers of the unemployed.

This deliberate stimulation to create self-employed jobs has manifested itself in two main ways. First of all, by making training opportunities more easily and widely available – as we saw in the previous chapter – and secondly, by offering those willing to take the plunge into self-employment free, but limited, financial support. Additionally, the Government has sought to help people go into business for themselves by guaranteeing loans on their behalf.

The first scheme we will now look at is a natural sequel to the previous chapter.

BUSINESS SUCCESS ALLOWANCE

This is part of the Business and Enterprise Services for the Unemployed provided by local Training and Enterprise Councils. These services are offered to those who are unemployed but want to become self-employed or set up their own business. Originally the scheme was known as the Enterprise Allowance Scheme, but its name was changed some three years ago. And, just to make matters more confusing, the same scheme may also be known in some areas as the Business Start-Up Scheme. But whatever its local name, what's on offer will remain broadly the same and follow these guidelines:

a) **Enterprise Awareness Events**. These events, often a day long, are meant to help you think about what it means to be self-employed.

b) **Business Advice and Counselling**. Just what it says, a way of pointing you towards various sources of support that you may need to start up and run your own business.

c) **Business Planning**. Help in sorting out financial planning and, according to the Employment Department, this will "reassure your bank manager or other backers". A free planning kit is part of this service.

d) **Business Training.** Short part-time courses to help you go into business for yourself. Most of these are free although you may have to pay towards the cost of some of them.

e) And, at the end of all this, you may qualify for the big prize, the **Business Success Allowance.** This is the one that actually puts money in your pocket, but see questions and answers below.

All the services listed above are provided by your local TEC and your initial contact will be your Jobcentre.

QUESTIONS AND ANSWERS ON BUSINESS SUCCESS ALLOWANCE

Q: Who is eligible for this Allowance?

A: The specific details – and even the name of the Allowance – may vary in different localities, but generally there are several conditions you have to meet in the first instance: 1) you must have been out of work for at least six weeks, although there are some exceptions to this rule; 2) you must be at least 18 years and under 65 years of age; 3) you must have at least £1,000 available to invest in your business but this amount can also be in the form of an agreed loan or overdraft; 4) you must intend to work full time, that is at least 36 hours a week, in your business; and 5) the intended business must be new and suitable for financial support.

Q: How much do I get?

A: This varies from area to area as the Allowances are granted on a discretionary basis. It used to be that you would have received £40 a week for a year (or £2,080 altogether); nowadays it's more likely to be something like £50 a week for 26 weeks (or £1,300). But check with your local TEC about exactly what is available in your area.

Q: Can any kind of business qualify?

A: No, there are several kinds of businesses which will not be eligible for support and these include: the promotion of particular political or religious views; gambling; sex or pornography; anything to do with obscene material; clairvoyance, astrology, psychic consultancies and other similar enterprises. Other businesses that may not be supported include: acting, musicians, singers and other entertainers; artists, sculptors and photographers; authors; medical and alternative medicine services; child-minders and crèches; taxi drivers; and franchise holders.

Q: Can I get the Allowance to expand an existing business?
A: No, the enterprise must be new and your application will be rejected if before the day it is received, you have already started up. What is meant by having 'started up' covers a wide area and includes such things as having advertised the goods or services you intend to provide; having engaged staff; having entered into contracts for the supply of goods or materials; or 'made any serious attempt before your application to generate a sales market'.

Q: How is the money paid?
A: This may vary, but generally it is paid once a fortnight in arrears. It is often a condition of the Allowance being granted that the money be paid into a specific business account.

Q: Does this Allowance stop me from getting other benefits?
A: Yes, it certainly does because, for starters, you would no longer be unemployed, but self-employed. Benefits that you would normally be entitled to as a self-employed person will generally not be affected, but check beforehand with your local Benefits Agency office as to how your entitlement to other benefits might be affected.

As can be seen from the above, the Allowance offers comparatively little money, but it does so as a grant and you don't have to repay it. The next scheme can, however, provide much larger sums to get you started.

THE LOAN GUARANTEE SCHEME

This is also operated by the Employment Department who describe it as "help for small firms with viable business proposals to obtain a supply of finance after their efforts to obtain conventional loans have proved fruitless, due perhaps to a lack of security or track record".

What the scheme does is reduce the lender's risk by providing a Government guarantee against default by borrowers. This guarantee only covers 85% of the loan and while the lender is indemnified, the borrower is not because they remain liable and recovery of the full debt may be sought. What this means is that a bank may be more willing to lend you the money because of the 85% guarantee, but you're still taking on the risk yourself. Having said that, it must be added that it can be an excellent way of raising money and the Employment Department point out that well-known names such as the Sock Shop chain and Waterstone's bookshops got off the ground by using the scheme.

Whatever its potential drawbacks, the scheme has certainly proven popular and, since its launch in 1981, has been used by more than 34,689 small firms for loans totalling over £1,000 million.

Some of the main points of the scheme are:

a) It is intended to be in addition to normal commercial finance, not in competition with it. So, it's not available if conventional finance can be obtained.

b) In return for the guarantee, a premium of 1.5% a year on the total loan (if it is based on variable rate lending) is payable by the borrower; for fixed rate lending, the premium payment is 0.5% a year on the whole loan. In specially designated areas – such as Inner City Task Force and City Challenge Areas – the premium payment is 0.5% on the whole loan for both fixed and variable rate lending.

c) All commercial decisions affecting the borrower are taken by the lender and the Department cannot intervene as its sole role is to check that the borrowers and their businesses are eligible for the scheme.

QUESTIONS AND ANSWERS ON THE LOAN GUARANTEE SCHEME

Q: How big can a loan be under the scheme?
A: Guarantees may cover loans up to £250,000 and a borrower may have more than one loan up to this limit.

Q: How long are the loans available for?
A: They are meant to cover medium-term loans of between two and seven years.

Q: Who is eligible?
A: Eligible businesses are sole traders (for example, the man

setting up on his own), partnerships, franchises, co-operatives and limited companies. These may either be already trading or about to start doing so.

Q: Are some kinds of businesses barred from the scheme?

A: Yes, quite a few business activities are not eligible and these include: agriculture and horticulture; authors, composers and certain other artists; banking, finance and other similar services; betting and gambling; forestry; house and estate agents; insurance and associated services; night clubs; and travel agents.

How to apply and for more information. Contact the *DTI, Small Firms Policy Branch, Loan Guarantee Section, St Mary's House, c/o Moorfoot, Sheffield S1 4PQ (Telephone: 0742-597308)* who will send you an information pack containing a list of the lenders – mainly High Street banks – who operate the scheme.

The next schemes we now look at are not Government funded and as such would normally fall outside the scope of this book. However, as their activities match so closely those described above, it seemed right to include a brief mention.

THE PRINCE'S YOUTH BUSINESS TRUST

This organisation can provide loans of up to £5,000 and bursaries (non-repayable grants) of up to £1,500 for young people trying to set up in business. You have to be aged between 18 and 25 (or between 18 and 30 for people with disabilities). You can get more information from: *PYBT, 5 Cleveland Place, London SW1 6JJ (Telephone: 071-321 6500)* or, if you live in Scotland, from: *The Prince's Scottish Youth Business Trust, Mercantile Chambers, 6th Floor, 53 Bothwell Street, Glasgow G2 6TS (Telephone: 041-248 4999)*.

LIVEWIRE

Sponsored by Shell UK, Livewire provides more than £150,000 worth of cash awards and help in kind every year for young people, aged 16 to 25, who want to set up their own businesses. The awards are made on the basis of plans submitted to judging panels and the top award is £3,000. More information from: *Livewire, FREEPOST, Newcastle-upon-Tyne NE1 1BR (Telephone: 091-261 5584)*.

11 How To Collect Housing And Other Associated Benefits

There are many benefits connected with housing and these cover all sorts of contingencies, including help with Rent and Council Tax as well as grants for repairs to your home. We will begin by looking at two of these benefits together.

HOUSING BENEFIT AND COUNCIL TAX BENEFIT

We have linked these benefits together because you apply for both of them in the same way. But, first of all, let us look at some figures.

Housing Benefit is one of the more expensive programmes and in 1992/93 was paid out to more than four million claimants at a total cost of £7.3 billion. Of this, £4,445 million went to 3,105,000 council tenants and £2,903 million was received by 1,210,000 private tenants. Council Tax Benefit is also a big spending programme and in 1993/94 was estimated to have cost £1.8 billion to provide assistance to more than five million households.

You can get Housing Benefit and Council Tax Benefit (hereafter referred to as HB and CTB respectively) if you have either rent to pay or are liable to pay the Council Tax and are on a low enough income to qualify. Says the DSS: "It makes no difference if you are in work or not, or whether you have paid any National Insurance contributions. Neither does it make any difference whether you have a partner or are single; live alone or with other people; or are a pensioner. However, if you have entered the UK from abroad, your entitlement to HB and CTB may be affected."

The CTB scheme also offers another type of help called 'second adult rebate' and this applies where there is a second adult in the household who would normally be expected to contribute towards the liable person's bill, but cannot afford to do so. It's important to be aware that these second adult rebates are not dependent upon the financial circumstances of the liable tax payer, but on those of the second adult. The rebates can be awarded to people who are solely liable – or treated as such – to pay the Council Tax and have another adult living with them, on a non-commercial basis, who is on a low income.

There are also special provisions for students, and properties occupied solely by students are exempt from Council Tax. This exemption applies equally to all such properties, whether rented or being bought, and to halls of residence. Therefore, most students will not be liable to pay Council Tax. However, certain students may be liable for the tax – for example, if they share their home with others who are not students. Where students have a liability to pay tax, they will be able to claim CTB if they are:

a) So-called 'vulnerable' students, a category that includes, for example, disabled students and also those who are lone parents.

b) Part-time students.

A partner, who is not a student, may claim CTB, and students may also qualify for second adult rebates. As far as HB is concerned, most full-time students are excluded from claiming this, but there are exceptions to this rule for students who are disabled as well as those with dependant children. If you are in either of these categories, you should check with your local council for more details.

It needs to be added that it doesn't matter what kind of rented premises you live in as HB is available for those in council housing, private rented accommodation, hotels, hostels, guest houses as well as many other types of rented accommodation.

What do the benefits provide? HB is meant to help with the part of the rent that you pay to live in your home. This amount is called the 'eligible rent' and may not be the same as you pay your landlord because your total rent may include things such as water charges, fuel costs and so on. However, you may also get help with some service charges such as those covering children's play areas, lifts, the cleaning of shared areas and so on. CTB is a rebate scheme that provides help towards your Council Tax.

How much do you get? Depending upon your income and savings, you could get up to 100% of your eligible rent from HB and up to 100% of your Council Tax liability. The maximum second adult rebate is 25%.

The amounts you may get are worked out by your local council and there are two different ways of approaching this:

a) If you are receiving Income Support, you will normally get the maximum benefit available.

b) If you're not already getting Income Support, your claim will be worked out on the basis of your average weekly income as well as taking into account any savings you may have. The rules regarding savings are broadly the same as for Income Support – see **Appendix A – Common Rules** at the back of this book. It is still possible that you may qualify for maximum benefit but it is more likely that the eventual benefit will be somewhat less than that. As with the Income Support calculation, your benefit will be reduced according to what extent your income exceeds your needs – the so-called 'applicable amount'. If your income is greater than the applicable amount, your benefit is reduced by a 'taper adjustment' of 65% for rent and 20% for Council Tax. That is to say that your maximum HB is reduced by 65p for each pound that your income exceeds the applicable amount, while your maximum CTB is reduced by 20p for each pound that your income exceeds the applicable amount.

Although the rates used to work out your benefit are generally the same as those for Income Support – see **Chapter 3 – How To Collect Income Support** – there are some differences in the allowances and premiums. These exceptions are shown below as weekly amounts.

Deductions for non-dependants living with you

For HB, there are four different rates:

☐ The lower rate of £5.00 for non-dependants aged 25 and over, in receipt of Income Support, or aged 18 and over, not in remunerative work, or with a gross income under £72.

☐ £9.00 for gross income from £72.00 to £107.99.

☐ £13.00 for gross income from £108.00 to £138.99.

☐ £25.00 for gross income of £139.00 or more.

For CTB, there are two rates for non-dependants aged 18 or over and in remunerative work:

☐ £2.30 for gross income of £108 or more.

☐ £1.15 for gross income up to £108.

Personal Allowance (for HB only). Single people aged 16 to 24 or lone parents aged 16 to 17 – £36.15.

Lone Parent Premium – £11.25.

Meals Deductions (the first figure is for an adult, the second for a child under 16). Full board – £16.30, £8.25; part board – £10.80, £5.45; breakfast only – £1.95, the same for an adult or a child.

Fuel charge deductions. Heating – £8.60; hot water – £1.05; lighting – £0.70; cooking – £1.05; total maximum fuel deduction – £11.40. If only one room occupied by non-dependant: heating and any hot water or lighting – £5.18; cooking – £1.05.

How to claim. There are two different ways to claim HB and CTB:

☐ If you're making a claim for Income Support, you will find *claim forms NHB1 (HB)* and *NHB1 (CTB)* inside the Income Support claim form you get from the DSS. These two forms should be returned to your local DSS office who will pass them on to your local council informing them at the time whether you're entitled to Income Support or not.

☐ If you're not claiming Income Support, make your claim for HB and CTB directly to your local council. Local councils have their own claim forms which may vary somewhat in contents, although the rules applied to your claim will be the same wherever you live.

If your claim is approved, there are several different ways in which Housing Benefit could be paid. If you're a council tenant, you'll receive your HB in the form of a rent rebate which simply means that your bill will be reduced. If you're a private tenant, the benefit payment will normally be sent directly to you or in certain instances to your landlord if you either request this or there are rent arrears of more than eight weeks.

Your Council Tax Benefit will normally be credited to you by the council sending you a Council Tax bill from which it has already been deducted.

For more information. See DSS *booklet RR2 – A Guide to Housing Benefit and Council Tax Benefit* or *leaflets RR1 – Housing Benefit* and *CTB1 – Help with the Council Tax.*

QUESTIONS AND ANSWERS ON HOUSING BENEFIT AND COUNCIL TAX BENEFIT

Q: Does it matter how much my rent is?

A: Yes, because if the council thinks your home is larger than it needs to be or is unreasonably expensive, it may restrict your eligible rent which usually means less HB. However, the council must make 'a realistic comparison that takes into account the needs of your household'. Certain people may be exempt from these rent restrictions if they fall into one of the vulnerable groups listed below, unless there is suitable alternative accommodation and it is reasonable to expect the claimant to move: aged 60 or over; incapable of work because of sickness or disability; or responsible for a child or young person who is a member of the same household.

Q: What happens when my landlord puts up the rent?
A: Your council may decide not to include a rent increase in your benefit if it is unreasonably high, but it must also consider the general level of increases locally.

Q: How long can the council take to decide on my claim?
A: Your claim for HB/CTB should be dealt with within 14 days of the council receiving all the information.

Q: For how long are the benefits payable?
A: Your local council will award benefit for a set period which can be anything up to 60 weeks. You will normally get a letter from the council asking you to renew your claim towards the end of the current period. If your circumstances change in a way that affects the benefits, you must tell your council as it may affect how much you receive.

The benefits above, although administered by local councils, are all Social Security benefits. But there are other sources of housing-related benefits and we will now look at ...

HOUSE RENOVATION GRANTS

The aim of the renovation grants system – which is overseen by the Department of the Environment – is to provide financial help for those who can least afford to pay for necessary work to be carried out on their homes. This means that the amount you may get will be decided by a test of your financial resources which will be explained in greater detail later together with details on how to apply. But, first of all, let us look at what kind of grants are available.

Renovation Grants. To be able to apply for these you must be or will be either the owner-occupier of the property or its landlord who is letting it on a residential basis. You can also apply for this grant if you are a tenant who is specifically responsible under the terms of your lease or tenancy agreement for carrying out the work. The main purposes of the grants include:

a) To bring the property up to the standard of fitness for human habitation, in which case the grant is mandatory for owner-occupiers and discretionary generally for landlords.

b) To repair or improve the property beyond the standard of fitness (for example, repairs to defective roofs, walls, floors; replacement of rotten windows, damp course, electric wiring, etc).

c) To provide insulation.

d) To provide heating.

e) For providing satisfactory internal arrangements – this could include altering such things as a staircase that is too steep; doorways that are too low; or a bathroom that can only be reached through a bedroom.

f) To create conversions, but there are usually various conditions attached to this. For example, you will be asked to prove that you intend to let out the newly created units.

Grants for most of these purposes, except for the first part of section a) above are discretionary, which means that your council does not have to award them, but may do so. The listed items are only examples of the kind of work for which a renovation grant may be available.

Common Parts Grants. These are meant to help with the improvement or repair of the common parts of buildings which contain one or more flats. Applications can usually be made by either the landlord alone or together with their tenants or by the tenants themselves providing that they are responsible for contributing towards the work in question.

The kind of work that is likely to qualify for a Common Parts Grant includes re-roofing, structural repairs and improvement to communal areas such as halls and staircases. These are, however, only examples and the works can be much more wide-ranging. Check with your council's renovation grants section.

HMO Grants. 'HMO' stands for 'houses in multiple occupation' where the occupants are not all part of the same household. These grants can only be applied for by the landlord and are available for works 'required to make an HMO fit for human habitation and to make it fit for the number of people living there'. Whether a house is fit for the number of occupants depends upon such things as cooking arrangements, food storage, washing and toilet facilities, and fire safety measures.

Disabled Facilities Grants. These grants are meant to help with the cost of making a home more suitable for a disabled person to live in and also to help the person manage more independently in the home. These grants can be applied for by: someone who is either registered – or could be registered – as disabled and is the owner-occupier or the tenant; or a landlord on behalf of a qualified tenant; or anyone who has a disabled person living in their home.

The council will also check whether the proposed works meet two conditions: 1) that they are necessary and appropriate to meet the needs of the disabled occupant; and 2) that they are reasonable and practicable taking into account the age and condition of the property.

If these conditions are met, a mandatory grant is available for works needed to provide better access in and out of the home; providing suitable bathroom and kitchen facilities; bringing the heating up to the necessary standard; improving access to various rooms within the home; and generally making provisions around the home which will help you cope better with your disability.

Apart from the above, a discretionary grant may be available for a wider range of other works which will help make a home more suitable for a disabled person's accommodation, welfare or employment.

Minor Works Assistance. This grant is always discretionary and is restricted to owner-occupiers and tenants who are receiving an income-related benefit. You can apply if you or your partner receive Income Support, Family Credit, Housing Benefit, Council Tax Benefit or Disability Working Allowance. These grants are, however, not available to either landlords or council tenants.

The main reasons why a grant might be awarded are: 1) to provide or improve thermal insulation; 2) to repair, improve or adapt a property for the special needs of elderly occupants, aged 60 or older; 3) to adapt a home to enable an elderly resident, aged 60 or older, to stay or move in with you; 4) to carry out repairs to a property in a clearance area; 5) for lead pipe replacement.

There is a limitation to the amount you can claim under this scheme and that is currently set at £1,080 per application, although the council can pay up to £3,240 in relation to a single property over three years.

How to apply. You apply to your local council who will provide you with a special form. Once you've made a 'fully completed application', the council must give you their decision within six months.

How much do you get? This depends upon two factors. First of all, the actual cost of the work that needs to be done, which could range from a few hundred pounds to several thousands. Secondly, your own situation as the amount of grant you get is decided by a test of financial resources. There are two different tests – one for owner-occupiers and tenants, the other for landlords. There is also a maximum limit to mandatory Renovation Grants and this is currently £20,000.

The test for owner-occupiers and tenants consists of the council working out how much you are reckoned to be able to pay towards the cost of the works. The amount of the grant will be the difference between what you're able to afford yourself and the total cost of the eligible works. Once again, the test is broadly similar to that for Income Support with the difference that any 'excess income' over your 'needs' will be used to calculate the size of loan that you're reckoned to be able to afford to help finance the works. This so-called 'affordable loan' is then deducted from the cost and your grant will be the remainder.

The test is different for landlords and takes into account the cost of the works as well as the potential increase in rental values this would create. This assessment is then used to calculate what the landlord is reckoned to be able to finance themselves and this amount is deducted from the grant.

For more information. See House Renovation Grants, published by the Department of the Environment, and available from your local council.

HOME ENERGY EFFICIENCY SCHEME

If you are on a low income, disabled or over the age of 60, you may be able to get a Department of Energy grant under this scheme to provide draught-proofing for your home and/or loft insulation.

To qualify for a grant you must be the householder, tenant or home owner and either you or your spouse must be either over the age of 60 or getting at least one of the following benefits: Income Support, Council Tax Benefit, Housing Benefit, Family Credit or Disability Living Allowance.

How much do you get? You get the cost of the necessary work up to set limits. These are currently:

□ For *draught-proofing*, up to £128.50.

□ For *loft insulation*, up to £198.70.

□ For both *draught-proofing and loft insulation*, up to £305.

The work is normally carried out by either network installers or listed contractors or you may choose to do it yourself, in which case the grant will only cover the cost of the materials.

How to apply and for more information. Write to: *Energy Action Grants Agency, PO Box 1NG, Newcastle-upon-Tyne, NE99 2RP.* You can also phone them free of charge on *0800 181 667.*

12 How To Get Free Legal Assistance

You can get all kinds of free legal aid and advice courtesy of the Government. This assistance is controlled by the Legal Aid Board which reports back to the Lord Chancellor.

Legal Aid is a major area of Government spending and in 1992/93, the last year for which figures are currently available, cost the taxpayers £1,093 million, although its total budget was £1,328 million, the rest of the money having been recovered through contributions, statutory charges and costs. Of this total, £423 million were spent in providing help in criminal cases, including the duty solicitor scheme.

In the same year, the Board paid for more than three million 'acts of assistance' which is not quite the same as the number helped because some of these 'acts' helped more than one person and in other instances some people were assisted more than once.

First of all, here's how to find a solicitor who offers Legal Aid:

Ask at your local *Citizens' Advice Bureau*, law centre or advice bureau; look in the *Solicitors' Regional Directory* which you'll find in your local library; go to any solicitor's office where the Legal Aid sign is displayed (it is a schematic drawing of two seated people facing each other across a table with the caption 'Legal Aid'); if you live outside England or Wales write to the *Legal Aid Board, 29-37 Red Lion Street, London WC1R 4PN*.

We will now look at the various schemes provided under the auspices of Legal Aid.

LEGAL ADVICE AND ASSISTANCE

Previously known as the 'Green Form Scheme', Legal Advice and Assistance provides a means of getting help from a solicitor, including general advice, writing letters, getting a barrister's opinion and preparing a written case if you have to go before a tribunal. This help is available for most legal problems, such as divorce or maintenance and, under certain circumstances, the making of a will.

Says Legal Aid: "This scheme enables people of small or moderate means to get help from a solicitor free until the charges reach a total of two hours of work (or three hours when preparing a petition in a matrimonial case)."

Help under this scheme is means-tested and there are two tests to determine whether you are eligible:

The savings test: Add up all your savings (but exclude from this the value of your home, household furniture and 'the value of the thing that you want advice about'). From your total savings, deduct the following allowances for any dependants – partner, children, relatives – you may have: for one dependant, deduct £335; for two dependants, £535; for three dependants, £635; plus another £100 for each additional dependant. What is left after making these deductions is called your 'disposable capital' and you will be eligible if this does not exceed £1,000.

The income test: Subject to the capital rule explained above, you will be automatically eligible for free Legal Advice and Assistance if you are receiving one of the following benefits: Income Support, Family Credit or Disability Working Allowance.

If you're not getting one of these benefits, your solicitor will add up the actual income of yourself – and your partner, if you have one – for the past week and deduct from it: 1) Income Tax and National Insurance contributions; 2) £26.00 for your partner; 3) the following allowances for children and dependants – dependant children and relatives under 11, £15.65; between 11 and 15, £23.00; between 16 and 17, £27.50; and 18 and over, £36.15. What is left after making these deductions is called your 'disposable income' and you qualify under the income test if this is less than £70 a week.

In the past, people earning more than a set amount were required to pay a contribution. This has now been completely eliminated and if you qualify you will not be asked to pay any contribution out of your savings nor from your income.

However, you will be required to pay for the solicitor if money or property is recovered or preserved. For example, if your solicitor recovers £400 for you and his charges are £50, you will only get £350. There are, however, exceptions to this and this rule will not apply if the money or property recovered consists of any of the following: up to £2,500 in matrimonial settlements; the recovery of various benefits such as Sickness or Unemployment Benefit; awards made by the Employment Appeal Tribunal; or half of any redundancy payments.

ASSISTANCE BY WAY OF REPRESENTATION

This scheme (also known as ABWOR) covers the cost of a solicitor preparing your case and representing you in most civil cases in magistrates' courts and what are now known as Family Proceedings Courts. Eligible cases include separation, maintenance, residence/contact, paternity and defended adoptions. This scheme is also available to help patients appearing before Mental Review Tribunals and prisoners facing disciplinary charges before boards of visitors.

To qualify financially, you must pass the tests of savings and income as for Legal Advice and Assistance (see above) with one difference: even if you do not qualify for Legal Advice and Representation because of savings in excess of £1,000, you will still qualify for ABWOR if your savings (plus dependants' allowances) are no more than £3,000 or if you're getting Income Support. However, if your 'disposable income' falls between the lower limit of £63 and the upper limit of £153, you will be required to pay a contribution from your own funds, this contribution being based on a sliding scale and being worked out as being one third of disposable income over £63 every week from the time ABWOR is granted until either ABWOR is withdrawn or the case comes to an end. Here's an example of how this works out in practice: if your disposable income is £93, deduct £63 from this amount which leaves £30. Divide this last sum by three to arrive at £10 and that will be your weekly contribution.

Once again, if money or property is recovered, you may also have to pay towards the costs.

CIVIL LEGAL AID

Having had Legal Advice and Assistance over a legal problem, your solicitor may advise you that the case should be taken to court and that is where Civil Legal Aid comes in. It covers the work leading up to and including the court proceedings and your representation by a solicitor and, if need be, a barrister.

You may be eligible for Civil Legal Aid even if you weren't granted Legal Advice and Assistance because the savings limit is higher, although the rule on income is broadly the same. There are also various exceptions and conditions, but see below for further information.

Civil Legal Aid is designed to help with cases in: The House of

Lords, The High Court and Court of Appeal, County Courts (but not judgment summonses and certain matrimonial cases), Family Proceedings Courts, The Employment Appeal Tribunal, The Lands Appeal Tribunal, The Commons Commissioners and some cases in The Restrictive Practices Court. One big exception is that help will not be available for cases involving slander and libel.

To qualify for Civil Legal Aid, you need to qualify financially in the first instance and this will be decided by assessment officers of the Benefits Agency who specialise in Civil Legal Aid cases. Once again, this is done on the basis of taking into account your savings, income, dependants and needs. The formula for doing this is broadly similar to that used for Income Support with some differences and will result in a yearly amount which is called your 'disposable income', that is an amount that you are reckoned to have available after meeting all your basic needs.

If your so-called disposable income is £7,060 or less (£7,780 in the case of personal injuries claims), you will qualify on the basis of income, but you will have to pay a graduated contribution towards the cost of the case if that income is more than £2,382. Generally, the contribution you will be expected to make will be one thirty-sixth of the difference between the assessed disposable income and the lower limit, this amount being payable each month for the life of the case.

As indicated above, your savings are also taken into account and if your 'disposable capital' is less than £6,750 (£8,560 for personal injuries cases) you will qualify. However, you may still be granted Civil Legal Aid even though your capital is more than these limits if your case is likely to be expensive.

If your savings are more than £3,000, you may be asked to pay a contribution. This could be as much as the total of your savings above the £3,000 limit, but could be less than that especially in the case of pensioners who benefit from special disregards. Of course, should you win your case, the other side may well be ordered to pay your costs. The other side of that coin is that, should you lose, you may be ordered to pay your opponent's costs. This is a decision that is made by the court and will depend on your means as well as your conduct in connection with the dispute.

CRIMINAL LEGAL AID

As its name implies, this scheme is to offer help with cases involving criminal offences and it really consists of two separate parts. The first, which is a kind of legal first aid, is the *Duty Solicitor Scheme*, which the Legal Aid Board explains as follows:

"If the police question you about an offence – whether or not you have been arrested – you have a right to free legal advice. There is no means test for such advice. In some circumstances the police can delay but not stop you seeing a solicitor. Ask for a solicitor you know, the 24-hour duty solicitor or choose a solicitor from the list the police keep.

"If you have to go to the magistrate's court on a criminal offence there will often be a duty solicitor available either at the court or on call to give you free advice and representation on your first appearance. Again, there is no means test. Ask the court staff for the duty solicitor. It is best, if possible, to get advice before you go to court."

If you end up being charged with a criminal offence, you can apply for Criminal Legal Aid and this may pay for some or all of the following: the cost of a solicitor to prepare your defence before you go to court and to represent you there; the cost of a barrister, if required; advice on appeal against a verdict or sentence; and help so you can apply for bail.

How to apply. You should apply to the court that is dealing with your case as soon as possible after you have been charged with a criminal offence. The necessary forms will be supplied by the court and you will have to give full details of your income and savings.

Criminal Legal Aid will be granted by the court if it decides that it is in the 'interests of justice' that you should be legally represented and that you need help to pay the costs of the case.

You may be asked to pay a contribution as a condition of Criminal Legal Aid, but not if you're in receipt of Income Support, Family Credit or Disability Working Allowance, or if your disposable capital is less than £3,000 or if your disposable income is less than £46.00 a week. If you have savings or income in excess of those limits, you may be asked to make a contribution partly from income and/or partly from capital. The actual amount you will have to pay will be stated in a notice that will be sent to you by the court. If you don't want to pay these contributions, you can ask for Criminal Legal Aid to be stopped but you must tell the court and your solicitor immediately.

The schemes outlined above all come under the direction of the Legal Aid Board and you can get more information from them. They publish various booklets and leaflets, including: *A Practical Guide to Legal Aid, How to Get Free or Low Cost Legal Help, What to Do if You Get a Summons or Are Questioned by the Police,* and *Criminal Legal Aid at the Police Station and in Court.* You can get these from: *The Legal Aid Board, 29-37 Red Lion Street, London WC1R 4PN. (Telephone: 071-405 6991).*

OTHER FREE SCHEMES

Apart from Legal Aid, there are other schemes under which you can get limited legal advice for free. These are run by solicitors participating in 'marketing schemes' operated by the Law Society.

Essentially, what these amount to is that you can get a free interview lasting about half an hour or so with a solicitor during which time they will be able to tell whether you have a reasonable case, what the costs of pursuing the matter might be, and if you're likely to qualify for Legal Aid. There are currently three such schemes:

The Accident Line. This has evolved out of a similar previous scheme called Accident Legal Advice Service and is aimed at people who were harmed by an accident of any kind in which someone else might be to blame and who may be able to seek compensation for injuries, loss of wages, damages to clothing and so on. The new scheme, which is due to be launched in June 1994, will provide a Freephone number (*0500 192 939*) which victims can call to apply for their free consultation.

Lawyers for Your Business. This provides a free consultation with a solicitor for people in business. The interview, which will last at least half an hour, could cover all sorts of business-related matters, including grants, taxation, insurance, franchising, licences, employment law and so on. The solicitor will provide a free 'diagnosis', explaining what further help may be needed and the likely cost. The Law Society points out that there is no obligation on the client to take the matter any further, no matter what advice they may receive.

Union Law. This is described as a "new legal services scheme for Trade Unions members" and its scope includes all aspects of law except work-related matters which are dealt with under the existing arrangements that unions have. The scheme covers all members of TUC unions and can also provide a fixed price conveyance.

You can find out which solicitors offer these schemes by consulting the *Solicitors' Regional Directory* at your local library, asking your *Citizens' Advice Bureau*, or contacting *The Law Society, 50/52 Chancery Lane, London WC2A 1SX*.

THE LOCAL REFERRAL SCHEME

This is a completely revamped version of the former national *Fixed Fee Interview* which ended in June 1993. The new scheme works on the basis of members of the public usually being referred to a solicitor via a participating agency, such as the local CAB, Law Centre or other advice agency, under local arrangements formulated within national guidelines agreed by the Law Society and the National Association of Citizens' Advice Bureaux. Just how the scheme works varies widely from area to area, but it usually provides for an initial diagnostic interview which can be either free or chargeable at a low cost. For more details, contact your local advice agency.

13 How To Collect War Pensions And Benefits

If you suffered injury or disablement or contracted any diseases as part of serving in HM Forces (or as a civilian, Civil Defence worker or seaman in time of war) or are the widow or dependant of such a person, you may be entitled to War Pension and Allowances.

The ones we will cover in this chapter include War Disablement Pension, Allowances for War Disablement Pensioners, Priority for Medical Treatment, Help with Funeral Costs, War Widow's Pension, Allowances for War Widows and Pensions for Dependants.

The War Pensions scheme – and other allowances linked to it – are run by an agency of the Department of Social Security called, reasonably enough, the *War Pensions Agency*, which is located at *Norcross, near Blackpool*. Apart from administering the DSS War Pensions and Allowances, this Agency also runs the very useful War Pensioners' Welfare Service, the work of which is explained in detail at the end of this chapter.

The War Pensions scheme currently provides benefits to some 300,000 people at a total cost of more than £1,000 million, which works out at just over £3,000 a year for the average claimant.

The idea of providing pensions for those injured in war is hardly new and history shows that there has been some form of pension scheme for veterans as far back as 500 BC; and, in Elizabethan times, voluntary grants from Commanders of the Forces financed compensation for soldiers with extra help coming from monastic houses and endowments from the churches.

In more modern times, the history of War Pensions really started in 1914 when the War Office (for officers), the Chelsea Commissioners (for other ranks) and the Admiralty (for Naval officers and seamen) were given the responsibility for distributing a 25 shillings weekly pension for total disablement and various other benefits. This was followed by the creation of a Ministry of Pensions in 1917 which ran the schemes, apart from an interruption from 1921 to 1939 when the Service Authorities looked after them. The Ministry eventually became part of the Department of Health and Social Security in 1968 and, since the reorganisation of the DHSS in 1988, War Pensions and ancillary benefits have been administered by the DSS (through its new

War Pensions Agency since April 1st 1994).

OVERVIEW OF WAR PENSIONS

War Pensions are not just for those who served in wartime as members of other groups may also be entitled. You're likely to have a valid claim to a War Pension if you match one of the categories listed below:

a) You were injured or disabled because of service in HM Armed Forces between 1914 and 1921 or at any time after the 2nd of September 1939.

b) You were either a civilian or Civil Defence worker and your disablement was caused by a war injury or war risk injury sustained during the Second World War.

c) You were a merchant seaman (this term includes Mercantile Mariners, Naval Auxiliary and Coastguard personnel as well) and your disablement is directly attributable to a war injury, war risk injury or detention sustained during any of the following periods: 1914 to 1918; 1939 to 1945; or during the Falklands Conflict (1982) or the Gulf Conflict (1991).

d) You were injured or disabled because of service while a member of the Polish Forces serving under British command during the 1939 war or in the Polish Resettlement Forces (there is a special condition here that the claimant must not have been back to live permanently in Poland after the termination of his service and that a widow must not have been back to live permanently in Poland after her husband's death).

e) You were injured or disabled because of service in the Home Guard between May 21st 1940 and December 31st 1944, or between April 28th 1952 and July 31st 1957; or because of service in the Ulster Defence Regiment (UDR) between April 1st 1970 and June 30th 1992.

f) You are the widow, widower or dependant relative of someone who has died as a result of injuries or disabilities that would have made him or her eligible.

The above lists the main reasons why someone may be eligible and eligibility is the first barrier to cross. The next one is that of entitlement which is considered mainly by medical assessors, although there may also be some input from lay people.

For a claim to succeed under the entitlement section, it must be shown that the wound, injury or disablement is either attributable to service or that, if it existed before or arose during service, that it was and remains aggravated by service.

Some examples will clarify these conditions:

☐ In the case of wounds sustained in action, the entitlement is quite clear as it is directly attributable.

☐ The same thing goes for injuries sustained during an accident while on duty as once again the cause is attributable and therefore the entitlement is quite clear.

☐ Things become more difficult in the case of injuries received in an accident while off duty and it must then be decided if service was the cause; if it was, then entitlement will be granted.

☐ Entitlement can be even more difficult to prove when a disease, as compared to a wound or injury, is the cause of disability. To qualify, it must be shown that service conditions were responsible for the onset of the disease in the first instance.

If a claimant has been found to be both eligible and entitled, the next step is assessment which determines the extent of the disablement and thereby sets the amount of pension that will be paid.

Assessment is purely a medical decision and is expressed as a percentage in steps ranging up to 100%. In the case of comparatively low disablement – less than 20% – it is assessed in one of the three following bands: 1 to 5%; 6 to 14%; and 15 to 19%. And, what's more, within each of those three bands there is also a further decision which sets one of three periods of award. These are: temporary less than a year; temporary more than a year; and indeterminate duration.

The amount you will get is very dependent upon how severely disabled you are – for example, in the case of a private, the difference is more than £70 a week between 20% and 100% disablement. The basis upon which this percentage is calculated is by a doctor comparing your loss of physical ability or mental health resulting from your disability to that of a healthy person of the same age and sex.

Having covered the main aspects which determine eligibility, entitlement and assessment, let us now look at the main benefits potentially available.

WAR DISABLEMENT PENSION

This is paid to those who have been found to have a disablement ranging between 20% and 100%. Disablements assessed at less than 20% are usually paid as a single award called a 'gratuity' and are covered in the next section.

There are no time limits for claiming your War Disablement Pension, but the DSS does say "it may be easier to allow your claim if you apply within seven years of the end of your service or date you sustained a war injury or war risk injury". That's good advice and even better advice is to claim as soon as possible because payments are normally only made from the date of the claim and are only backdated in exceptional circumstances. However, a War Pension cannot be paid before the termination of service.

How much do you get? This varies greatly because it depends upon the assessed percentage of disablement. The full rates are listed in DSS *leaflet MPL154 – Rates of War Pensions and Allowances* which can be obtained from DSS offices. While it would be unreasonable to reproduce them all in this book, here are some typical examples of rates payable from April 11th 1994:

- ☐ 100% disablement – £98.90 a week.
- ☐ 50% disablement – £49.45 a week.
- ☐ 20% disablement – £19.78 a week.

WAR DISABLEMENT PENSION AWARDS (GRATUITIES)

As explained above, disablements of less than 20% are usually covered by a single payment. These vary according to the assessed degree of disablement, the estimated duration of the disablement and your rank in service.

How much do you get? Here are some examples of the single payment awards (please note that while Army ranks are used to illustrate the examples, the same rates apply to equivalent ranks in the Royal Navy or Royal Air Force):

Rank	Disablement %	Less than 1 year	More than 1 year	Indeterminate
Private	1 to 5%	£257	£515	£1,538
	6 to 14%	£573	£1,142	£3,417
	15 to 19%	£1,000	£1,997	£5,974

Rank	Disablement %	Less than 1 year	More than 1 year	Indeterminate
Lieutenant or second Lieutenant	1 to 5%	£260	£521	£1,562
	6 to 14%	£580	£1,156	£3,471
	15 to 19%	£1,013	£2,023	£6,074
Major General	1 to 5%	£269	£535	£1,614
	6 to 14%	£600	£1,195	£3,588
	15 to 19%	£1,047	£2,092	£6,278

It must, however, be noted that no award can be made for noise-induced sensorineural hearing loss which has been assessed at less than 20%.

GRATUITIES FOR SPECIFIED MINOR INJURIES

These cover primarily the loss of fingers and toes and the amount of the gratuity ranges from £4,703 for an officer who lost all of his index finger to £624 for a private who lost part of a big toe. Different scales apply for different fingers and toes as well as multiple losses and whether the claimant was an officer or not.

The above are the main provisions of the War Disablement Pension scheme, but there are also extra allowances which may be paid with a War Disablement Pension. These are:

Allowance for lowered standard of occupation. If your war pensioned disablement stops you from doing work that is equivalent to your pre-service occupation you qualify for this allowance. However, the allowance plus your pension must not add up to more than the 100% Disablement Pension.

The maximum payable under this allowance is £1,945 yearly for officers and £37.28 a week for other ranks.

Unemployability Supplement. This supplement may become payable if your disability has made you unemployable. Those receiving this may still be allowed to earn up to £2,236 a year, the amount varying according to the circumstances.

The basic personal Unemployability Supplement allowance is

£3,188 a year for an officer and £61.10 a week for other ranks. Additional allowances are made for adult dependants and children and there is a further Invalidity Allowance if the unemployability began before a certain age.

Constant Attendance Allowance. This may be payable at one of four rates if you need regular personal attendance because of your pensioned disablement and you are getting a War Disablement Pension at the 80% rate or higher.

This allowance is paid at one of four rates depending on the amount of care and attendance you need:

	Officers (yearly)	**Other ranks** (weekly)
Half day rate	£976	£18.70
Full day rate	£1,952	£37.40
Intermediate rate	£2,927	£56.10
Exceptional rate	£3,903	£74.80

You may get CAA at the highest rate if you're suffering from a terminal illness because of your pensioned disablement.

Comforts Allowance. This rather wonderfully titled allowance is something that can be claimed at the higher rate by those who are receiving Constant Attendance Allowance and Unemployability Supplement or those who are getting a 100% pension for very severe multiple disability as well as Constant Attendance Allowance. The higher rate payment is £835 a year for officers and £16.00 a week for other ranks.

There is also a lower rate of Comforts Allowance which pays £417 a year to officers and £8.00 a week to other ranks. This rate is paid to those who don't qualify for the higher rate but do get either Constant Attendance Allowance or Unemployability Supplement.

Exceptionally Severe Disablement Allowance. This allowance is payable if you get Constant Attendance Allowance permanently at one of the two highest rates, or would do but don't get it because you are in an NHS hospital or a home. There is one rate payable – £1,952 a year for officers and £37.40 a week for other ranks.

Severe Disablement Occupational Allowance. This allowance is payable to those receiving Constant Attendance Allowance at one of the two highest rates and who are normally in employment. There is one rate payable – £976 a year for officers and £18.70 a week for other ranks.

Clothing Allowance. This is a very democratic allowance because it is the same – £126 a year is the higher rate and £80 the lower rate – for both officers and other ranks. This may be payable if your pensioned disablement causes exceptional wear and tear on your clothes. For example, the higher allowance may be paid if you have more than one artificial limb, or a tilting-table limb.

Age Allowance. This allowance may be payable to those aged 65 or over and in receipt of a War Disablement Pension at the 40% rate or more. There are four rates payable depending on how disabled you are:

Disablement	Officers (yearly)	Other ranks (weekly)
40 to 50%	£344	£6.60
60 to 70%	£532	£10.20
80 to 90%	£759	£14.55
100%	£1,064	£20.40

Mobility Supplement. Once again this is the same for all ranks, £1,855 a year for officers and £35.55 a week for other ranks. To qualify you will need to be unable to walk – or virtually so – because of your pensioned disablement which must have been assessed at 20% or higher. You may also qualify if you are both blind and deaf and need the assistance of another person to get to a required destination while out of doors. If you qualify for Mobility Supplement, you won't have to pay vehicle excise duty and will be able to receive the orange badge which· gives car-parking concessions in the UK and some European countries.

Treatment Allowance. This may be payable if you're having treatment – either in hospital or at home – for a pensioned disablement as a result of which you lose earnings. The allowance is equal to a pension at the 100% disablement rate.

OTHER ENTITLEMENTS

Priority hospital treatment. If you need treatment for your pensioned disablement you should get priority in an NHS hospital before everyone except emergency or other urgent cases.

Private treatment. The Department can only pay for private treatment or a privately purchased appliance (such as an artificial limb or hearing aid) where this is necessary for the pensioned disablement and no suitable treatment, appliance or aid is available through the NHS. Prior approval must be obtained from the War Pensions Agency.

Hospital treatment expenses. These cover expenses incurred by the pensioner in obtaining treatment for the pensioned disablement (such as travel expenses, subsistence, loss of earnings in connection with attendance at hospital).

Convalescence breaks. Up to four weeks in a year may be approved where a severely disabled war pensioner is unable to take a holiday in a normal guest house or hotel accompanied by his carer because of the pensioned disablement *or* because of the state of a carer's health it is necessary for the carer to have a break.

Skilled nursing care. The Department may pay the fees at a suitable nursing home for a severely disabled war pensioner who requires skilled nursing care because of the accepted disablement.

Chiropody. The cost of private chiropody treatment may be met by the Department if the treatment is required for the pensioned disablement.

'Remedial' treatment. Where a pensioner suffers from a psychiatric condition as a pensioned disablement the Department may meet the costs of short-term treatment (for up to six weeks in a year) in a home run by the Ex-Services Mental Welfare Society.

House adaptation grants. These grants – up to £750 – are available to severely disabled war pensioners where the need for the adaptation results from the pensioned disablement.

HELP WITH FUNERAL COSTS

The funeral costs of a war pensioner may be claimed from the DSS providing one of the three following situations apply:
a) The cause of death was the result of the disability for which he or she had received the pension.
b) The war pensioner died in hospital while having treatment for

that disability.
c) The war pensioner was entitled to Constant Attendance Allowance at the time of death.

All of the above, of course, has been concerned with benefits which are meant for those who suffered service-connected disablement themselves. There are, however, also connected benefits for their dependants ...

WAR WIDOW'S PENSION

You may qualify for a War Widow's Pension if one of the following conditions is met:
a) Your husband's death was the result of service in the Armed Forces between 1914 and 1921 or at any time after September 2nd 1939; or your husband was a war pensioner receiving Constant Attendance Allowance when he died, or would have received it had he not been in hospital at the time.
b) Your husband was a civilian or Civil Defence worker and his death was the direct result of a war injury or a war service injury sustained during the Second World War.
c) Your husband was a merchant seaman (term includes Mercantile Mariners, Naval Auxiliary and Coastguard personnel as well) and his death was directly attributable to a war injury, war risk injury or detention sustained during any of the following periods: 1914 to 1918; 1939 to 1945; or during the Falklands Conflict (1982); or the Gulf Conflict (1991).
d) Your husband served as a member of the Polish Forces in the 1939 war under British command or in the Polish Resettlement Forces and his death was the result of service.
e) Your husband died as a result of service in the Home Guard between May 21st 1940 and December 31st 1944 or between April 28th 1952 and July 31st 1957.
f) Your husband died as a result of service in the Ulster Defence Regiment (UDR) between April 1st 1970 and June 30th 1992.
There are two rates of War Widow's Pension: the standard rate – which is higher than the National Insurance Widow's Pension – and the lower rate which is the one usually paid where the widow is under 40, and has no children or where she is unable to support herself.

How much do you get? The standard rate of War Widow's Pension ranges from £74.70 a week for the widow of a private to £4,163 a year for the widow of a Major-General.

There are additional allowances to the basic pension:

Age Allowance. Additional payments ranging up to £1,273 yearly are paid according to the age of the widow, starting at 65, and according to the rank of the deceased.

Children's Allowance. Up to £788 a year depending upon rank as above.

Rent Allowance. The same for all ranks with a maximum weekly rate of £28.25, this is available only to widows who maintain a home for a child.

Special Temporary Allowance for Widows. You may get this for 26 weeks after your husband's death if at the time of his death he was a war pensioner getting Constant Attendance Allowance or Unemployability Allowance. The amount you'll receive will roughly match his total War Pension and Allowances.

OTHER WAR PENSIONS

There are other War Pensions for special cases:

War Widower's Pension. A man who was financially dependent on his late wife may get this if her death was due to service and he hasn't got enough to live on. Maximum rates are £4,621 a year for a widower of an officer and £74.95 a week for a widower of any other rank.

Unmarried Dependants Who Live as Spouses. The conditions are the same as for war widows – see above.

Orphan's Pension. For orphans if a parent's death was due to service. The amounts range between £3,006 yearly for the adult infirm dependant of an officer to £15.50 weekly for the dependant of any other rank.

How to claim. All the above pensions and allowances should be claimed by writing in the first instance to: *War Pensions Agency, DSS, Norcross, Blackpool FY5 3WP.*

If you're claiming on your account, the following details will help speed matters along: your full name (including any previous names, maiden names, or previous married names); if you're claiming because of service in the Armed Forces also give your Service Number, Rank/Rating, branch of the Forces; Regiment or Corps, dates of enlistment and discharge (if you're not sure about any of these, give what information you can, but don't put off claiming); if you're claiming as a civilian or as a former member, for example, of the Merchant Navy, Civil Defence or National Fire Service, give as much information as you can about how and when you were injured or disabled.

If you're claiming as a widow, apply to the same address, giving your full name, your late husband's name and, if he had a War Pension, his reference number if you know it. If he did not have a War Pension, or if you do not know the reference number, give as many details of his service as you can. See the paragraph above for the sort of details you should try to provide.

Other claimants, such as war widowers, write to the same address, giving your full name, the full name of the deceased relative and the War Pension reference number if you know it; otherwise provide as many details of the deceased relative's service as you can. .Advice can be obtained by phone from the *War Pensions Helpline on 0253-858 858.*

For more information: See *leaflets FB16 – Sick or Injured through Service in the Armed Forces?, MPL152 – War Widows and other Dependants, MPL153 – Guide for the War Disabled*, and *MPL154 – Rates of War Pensions and Allowances.*

WAR PENSIONERS' WELFARE SERVICE

This is a most useful service available to help war pensioners and widows with their problems. Welfare Officers will see you in your own home and provide advice and information on a wide variety of matters, including money difficulties. Welfare Officers also work in close contact with local authority social services and voluntary organisations who might be able to offer additional help.

How to get in touch. Ask your local DSS office for the address of the nearest branch of the War Pensioners' Welfare Service or ask for *leaflet MPL153 – Guide for the War Disabled* which lists all local offices (currently on pages 24 to 26).

14 How To Collect Education Grants And Loans

There are two main sources of Government money for students – awards and loans which are administered in quite different ways. The other big difference, of course, is that the awards don't have to be repaid by the student whereas the loans do.

Current Government policy is gradually to increase the amount available as loans while keeping the grant awards at the same level. This will have the effect over a period of time of increasing the proportion of the total which is paid out as loans, thereby making students responsible for eventually paying a greater part of their education costs. For example, in the next two years to come – 1995/96 and 1996/97 – it is expected that the main grant rates will be reduced by about 10% a year, but that the loan rates will be increased to compensate for this. We will begin by looking at the awards first.

STUDENT GRANTS

'Award' is the technical term used to describe the money paid by your Local Education Authority (hereafter referred to as LEA) towards both your living costs, that's the 'grant' part, and the college bills for your tuition, or the fees. You don't usually get to see this second element as the LEA will generally pay the fees directly to the college. So the thing that directly concerns you is the grant because that is the bit that is paid to you.

The grant is paid on a means-tested basis, which means that there are standard scales for calculating how much you're entitled to; and how much you, your parents or your spouse will be expected to contribute towards this sum. Before going into this deeper, let us first clarify eligible courses and what conditions you need to meet personally to be eligible.

As a general rule, courses are eligible if they are:
a) Full-time, including so-called 'sandwich' courses; and
b) Are held in a UK university or other publicly funded college or certain specified private colleges; and
c) Lead to a University or Council for National Academic Awards

first degree; or a Diploma of Higher Education; or a Higher National Diploma; or a Postgraduate Certificate of Education; or a specified comparable qualification.

You, as a student, will be personally eligible if:

a) You meet the residence requirement which normally means that you must have been living in the British Isles for the past three years, although there are various exceptions to this; and

b) You've had no previous help from public funds while attending other higher education courses in the past. However, in many instances that previous help will be disregarded and you will still be eligible. The rules governing this are very complicated and if they affect you, you will need to consult your LEA.

If you are attending an eligible course and you are personally eligible as well, you are legally entitled to a *mandatory grant*.

If your course is eligible but you are not personally eligible, your LEA may choose to give you a *discretionary grant*. If it does, that grant will be at the same rates as a mandatory one.

If your course is not eligible, your LEA may give you a discretionary grant and can also decide how much it will be.

How much do you get? What you actually receive depends on two things – first of all, your maximum entitlement which consists of the basic rate of grant plus any additional allowances you may be able to claim; and, secondly, any contribution you, your parents or spouse may be calculated to be able to pay. This contribution will be deducted from your maximum entitlement.

How your maximum entitlement is worked out. First of all, you're entitled to the Basic Grant Rate that applies to you. For the academic year 1994/95 this is £2,560 if you're living away from the parental home and studying in London; £2,040 if you're living away from home and studying elsewhere than in London; and £1,615 if you're living at home. You may be able to get the 'away from home' rate if you are married; or if you live with your parents but they cannot support you because of age or incapacity; and for certain other reasons. If your circumstances are at all unusual, check with your LEA whether you might qualify for the higher rate.

Apart from the Basic Grant, you may be entitled to **Additional Allowances**. These are:

Extra Weeks Attendance. This is paid for each week you attend college in excess of 30 weeks and 3 days (25 weeks and 3 days for Oxford and Cambridge) – £74.05 in London; £55.45 elsewhere;

and £38.70 if you're living in the parental home.

Disabled Allowances. If your disability increases your travelling costs you may get an extra travel allowance. You may also receive other means-tested allowances: up to £4,730 a year towards a non-medical personal helper; up to £3,560 for the whole of your course towards major items of specialist equipment; up to £1,185 a year towards further expenditure. You'll normally be expected to meet part of your travelling expenses – the first £231 if you live at home or the first £149 if you live in hall or lodgings – from your grant and any loan.

Travelling Expenses. You can claim these if you are disabled; or must attend a place in the UK away from your main college as part of a medical, dental or nursing course; or you must attend an institution outside the UK as part of your course.

Maintaining a Home. If you have to maintain a home for yourself and a dependant in addition to the one from which you attend the course, you can claim an extra £595 a year.

Older Students. If you are 26 or over and have earned, or received in taxable Unemployment or Supplementary Benefits or Income Support, at least £12,000 in total during the three years before the start of your course, you are eligible for an extra allowance which currently is: if you're 26 at the start of the course – £300; aged 27 – £535; aged 29 – £800; or aged 29 or older – £1,045.

Dependants. You may be able to claim extra if you have dependants. What you will get will be affected by any income these may have and the current maximum amounts you can get are: spouse or other adult dependant (or first child if no adult dependant) – £1,820; children – under 11 – £385; 11 to 15 – £765; 16 to 17 – £1,010; 18 and older – £1,460.

All of the amounts listed above that are applicable to your circumstances make up your maximum entitlement. However, what you will actually get is subject to the contributions that you, your parents or your spouse may be expected to make as that amount will be deducted from your entitlement.

The calculation of this expected contribution is very complicated and outside the scope of this book but fuller details of it can be found in *Student Grants and Loans*, published by the Department of Education and Science, which you can get from your local LEA. However, broadly speaking, your grant will be reduced if: a) your own income exceeds certain limits; or b) your parents' or spouse's 'residual' income, that is what is left after making allowances for their needs, is higher than set amounts. The amount by which your grant will be reduced is on a sliding scale.

How to apply. You need only make one application to cover your whole course and application forms can be obtained from your LEA, although most schools should also have them. It's best to apply as soon as possible, but not before January for a course starting the following autumn. There is no need to wait until you've been accepted for the course although you will have to supply evidence of acceptance later.

STUDENT LOANS

Loans are a way of topping up the grant to meet day-to-day living expenses and were introduced in 1990 when they were described as "a means of sharing student support more equitably between students, taxpayers and parents".

Students, of course, are free to decide whether or not to take up a loan and how much they wish to borrow, that is up to the maximums specified.

As with the Basic Grant, the amount you can borrow is linked to where you live and study. These are the maximum facilities for 1994/95:

☐ Students living in London and away from the parental home: full year rate – £1,375; final year rate – £1,005.

☐ Students living away from home elsewhere than London: full – £1,150; final – £840.

☐ Students living at the parental home: full – £915; final – £670.

Unlike grants, loans are not means-tested but you have to meet the same residence requirements as for grants. Additionally, you must be aged less than 50 years and also hold a bank or building society account.

You will not be asked to start repaying your loan until the April after you finish or leave your course and the repayments will be made in a fixed number of monthly instalments which is currently £60 for most borrowers and £84 for those who obtained loans for five academic years or more. Borrowers may, however, repay more quickly than that if they wish.

The amount you have to repay will be increased by the application of 'indexation' during the lifetime of the loan. Indexation means that the amount you owe is linked to inflation with the net result that the value of what you have to pay back will be more or less the same as the value of what you borrowed at the time the loan was made.

Repayment of your loan may be deferred if your income when you start work is below 85% of national average earnings. While payments are being deferred, the amount oustanding will still be subject to indexation. Any outstanding loan will be cancelled in the event of your death.

How to apply. You can only apply for your loan once you're actually attending your course and your college will be able to supply the necessary forms. If your course lasts more than one year you will need to apply each year you wish to receive a loan.

When you ask for the application form at your college, they will check whether you're eligible and, if you are, issue an eligibility certificate. Once you've completed the application, it should be sent to: *Student Loans Company Limited, 100 Bothwell Street, Glasgow G2 7JD*. You can also get more information from them by asking for their *leaflet The Student Loans Scheme* or by phoning them on *0345-300 900*, calls to this number being charged at the local rate.

ACCESS FUNDS

Access Funds are distributed to colleges so they can help students who 'for whatever reasons, face financial difficulties or where access to higher or further education might be inhibited by financial considerations.'

The individual colleges are responsible for deciding which students should receive payments and how much these payments might be, so what is available will vary considerably across the country. For further details you should ask at your college where usually the student support or student services office will deal with Access Funds enquiries.

OTHER SOURCES

Certain students may be able to get assistance from a scheme designed to stimulate co-operation in the EC and run by the European Community Action Programme for Education and Training for Technology (known as COMETT). Further information is available from your university.

BURSARIES

ERASMUS is the European Action Scheme for the Mobility of University Students and may be able to offer a grant towards the increased costs of study elsewhere in the EC. More information is available from: *UK ERASMUS Student Grants Council, The University, Canterbury, Kent CT2 7PD.*

LINGUA is an EC programme designed to improve the quality of teaching and learning of foreign languages, and students following courses in which foreign languages are a major component may be able to get a grant. You can get more information by writing to LINGUA at the same address as shown for ERASMUS above.

Certain students on initial teaching trainer courses for secondary school teaching may be able to get special tax-free bursaries, student awards and loans. For more information, contact: *DFE, Teachers' Branch (TQ), Mowden Hall, Staindrop Road, Darlington, Co Durham DL3 9BG*; or from: *Teaching as a Career, Sanctuary Buildings, Great Smith Street, London SW1P 3BT.*

The Open University says that "substantial help with fees might be available to students who were registered as being unemployed for at least six weeks and to students from low income households" and also that "many employers sponsor students, specially in the Open Business School". You can get more details from: *Central Enquiry Service, The Open University, PO Box 200, Milton Keynes MK7 6YZ.*

15 How To Collect Retirement Pension

The State Retirement Pension scheme has the biggest pay out of all Social Security programmes and last year it spent £28,052 million to provide for an average of 9,821,000 recipients at any given time.

Major changes are being planned in how retirement pensions will be paid out in the future and the current Government has published proposals that will make the pensionable age the same for both men and women. At the moment, men become eligible for their state pension when they reach the age of 65 years, while women get theirs five years sooner at the age of 60. Under the proposals – and it must be stressed that is all they are for the time being as they are subject to Parliamentary approval – it is suggested that the following changes be made:

1) The state pensions will be equalised at age 65 for both men and women as of April 6th 2020, the change from 60 to 65 for women being phased in over the ten-year period from 2010 to 2020.

2) That National Insurance contributions, counting towards both the basic and the additional earnings-related pension, would be payable until state pension age.

3) That as of 2010, the current arrangement which gives National Insurance credits to men who are not working or do not pay National Insurance contributions between the age of 60 and state pension age, would also be extended to women.

4) That the arrangement under which married women can currently get a pension because of their husband's National Insurance contributions would also be extended to men to give them the same right in regards to contributions paid by wives.

5) That the extra pension that can be claimed for dependants would be the same for men and women as of 2010.

If Parliament eventually approves these proposals, the gradual phasing in of the changes would mean that:

☐ Women who were born before April 6th 1950 would not be affected and they would still get their state pension when they reached the age of 60.

☐ Women with birthdates between April 6th 1950 and April 5th 1955 would reach state pension age between 60 and 65, the exact age being determined by a sliding scale that would gradually set pensionable age later for those born later. In other words, the younger you are now, the longer the extra time you will have to wait for your pension.

☐ Women born on or after April 6th 1955 would not be able to get their state pension until the age of 65.

Although these proposals have been put forward under the basis of 'equalising' state pension age for men and women – something which at first glance perhaps appears only fair – there can be little doubt that the main underlying reason for them is eventually to reduce the burden that state pensions place on the overall social security system. It yet remains to be seen whether the proposed measures become law in due course, especially as some very strong opposition to them has already been voiced.

In the meantime, it is obviously good advice that younger women should think about their pensions provisions as they will have to wait five years longer than anticipated for the one from the state.

The above is, of course, a long way in the future. For the time being, to be able to claim Retirement Pension, you must meet two conditions in the first instance:

a) You must have reached state pensionable age, which as already stated is currently 60 for a woman and 65 for a man.

b) You must have met the National Insurance contributions and/or earnings conditions. But more about these later.

Two major elements combine to make up your Retirement Pension: the so-called Basic Pension and the Additional Pension. On top of that, you may be entitled to various additions, such as Graduated Pension, Invalidity Addition, Age Addition and Extra Pension for Dependants.

We will begin by looking at the major components first of all.

BASIC PENSION

How much Basic Pension you may get is governed by how many qualifying years you have in your NI contributions record. However, if you haven't got enough qualifying years in your working life to get the full rate – or 100% – of the Basic Pension, you may be able to claim a reduced one. Additionally, you may also be able to pay off some arrears of contributions to get more qualifying years and thereby increase the percentage of Basic Pension you'll receive.

NI Class 1 (employee), Class 2 (self-employed) and Class 3

(voluntary) contributions that you have paid during your working life all count towards Basic Pension.

The percentage of Basic Pension you'll get is based on a table which links the number of years in your working life to the number of qualifying years during which you have paid sufficient NI contributions.

For example, someone with a working life of 31 years and a record of 27 qualifying years would get 100%. But the same person with a working life of 36 years of which still only 27 were qualifying years would only get an 85% pension. On the other hand, someone with a working life of 49 years would need at least 44 qualifying years to get the maximum rate. Generally, you will qualify for a full Basic Pension if you have qualifying years for about 90% of your working life.

In effect, the percentage of Basic Pension you'll get is not matched so much to how much you have paid in but rather to what percentage of your working life you have paid sufficient NI contributions.

The entitlement table goes down in steps of two or three per cent until it reaches 25% – below that no Basic Pension will be payable at all. To qualify for the minimum Basic Pension, you usually need at least 9 or 10 qualifying years.

If you think that you won't have enough contributions to qualify (we'll show you later how to find out and get a forecast of your pension), it may be possible to pay Class 3 contributions for previous years which will enable you to qualify for a Basic Pension at the minimum rate or to increase the percentage of Basic Pension for which you have already qualified. If you want to know whether this is possible in your case, ask at your local DSS office.

Married women who are not entitled to a pension on their own contribution record may get a pension on their husband's contributions and there are special rules for people who have been divorced or widowed.

How much do you get? These are the current 100% weekly rates (remember your entitlement may be less than that because of your contributions record): single person, man or woman on the basis of their own contributions or late spouse's contributions – £57.60. There are also extras payable for dependants and you can get additional payments of £9.80 for the first child and £11.00 for other children for whom you're entitled to Child Benefit.

You can also claim an extra pension of £34.50 for one of the following adult dependants: 1) your wife unless she already gets Basic Pension (or some other benefit) of at least the amount of the extra pension; 2) your husband, provided you were entitled to an increase of Sickness Benefit, Unemployment Benefit or Invalidity Benefit for him immediately before you qualified for your pension; 3) someone who looks after a child or children for whom you're entitled to get Child Benefit.

But you will not be able to get the dependant addition for an adult living with you and falling in one of the categories above who is earning more than, or getting an occupational pension, of more than £45.45 a week. If the adult dependant does not live with you this income limit is reduced to £34.50.

If you get a reduced Basic Pension, these extras – apart from the one for children – will also be reduced accordingly.

ADDITIONAL PENSION

This is an earnings-related part of your pension – also known as SERPS – and the amount that you will get depends upon your earnings as an employee since April 1978 on which you paid Class 1 contributions (Class 2 self-employed contributions are also counted for this). The amount is highly variable and you'll see further on how you can get a forecast of your future entitlement.

GRADUATED PENSION

This is another possible addition to your Basic Pension and is related to the amount of graduated NI contributions you paid between April 1961 and April 1975 when the Graduated Pension scheme was in existence. This Graduated Pension remains payable even if you are not entitled to either Basic or Additional Pension.

The amount you will get depends on the number of units of graduated contributions you paid in the relevant period. To work out the number of units, you have to add together all your graduated contributions, divide the total by 9 for a woman, and 7.5 for a man, and round up any odd half unit, ignoring less than half a unit. To find the rate payable, multiply the number of units by the unit value in force when you retire – currently this is 7.48 pence weekly.

OVER 80s PENSION AND AGE ADDITION

When you reach the age of 80, your retirement pension will be increased by an 'age addition' which is currently £0.25 weekly. There is usually no need to claim this as your payment should be adjusted automatically. However, should this not happen you should contact your local DSS office.

There is also a special provision – called the Over 80s Pension – for people who reach the age of 80 and who are either not getting any state retirement pension (for example, because they hadn't paid any National Insurance contributions) or are getting one that is less than the amount payable on a spouse's contributions. Apart from the age requirement, you must also have lived in the United Kingdom for at least ten years since you reached the age of 60. Even if your situation doesn't quite match this residency condition, it may still be worth applying because time spent in a European Community country may count towards your entitlement to this benefit.

The current full rate for the Over 80s Pension is £33.70 a week and it is being paid out to 30,000 beneficiaries at a total yearly cost of £36 million, which works out at an average of £1,200 yearly per claimant.

For more information. See DSS *leaflet N1 184 – Over 80s Pension.*

INVALIDITY ALLOWANCE

You can get this if you had an Invalidity Allowance shortly before you reached state pensionable age. The total of any Additional Pension payable and contracted out deduction will be taken away from your Invalidity Allowance and you will get any balance left over. The current rates of Invalidity Allowance can be found in **Chapter 6 – How to Collect Invalidity and Disability Benefits**.

How to claim. Normally you will automatically be sent *claim form BR1* about four months before you reach pension age. If, however, you haven't received this within a month or so of the time it is due, enquire at your DSS office. Men will receive two claim forms so that, if they are married, their wives can also claim.

Complete the form as soon as possible and return it to the address shown on it. If you choose not to claim your pension at this time

– see below – you will be sent another one when you near age 65 or 70 or you can get one any time from the DSS.

For more information. See DSS *leaflets FB6 – Retiring?, NP46 – A Guide to Retirement Pensions,* and *FB32 – Benefits after Retirement.*

QUESTIONS AND ANSWERS ON PENSIONS

Q: How do I get a forecast of my future pension entitlement?

A: There are two different kinds of forecasts that you can get on request if you are either a woman under the age of 59 years and 8 months or a man under the age of 64 years and 8 months: 1) a forecast of both your Basic Pension and Additional Pension can be obtained by getting *form BR19* from the DSS and, after completing it, returning it to the address shown on the form; or 2) if you just want a forecast of your Additional Pension, get *leaflet NP38 – Your Future Pension* and use the form it contains.

Q: Do I have to claim my pension when I reach pensionable age?

A: No, and you can in fact 'earn' extra entitlements – called 'increments' – if you put off receiving your pension. But you can only earn these increments if you postpone your pension for at least seven weeks and only until you reach 65, if you're a woman, or 70, if you're a man. For every six days that you postpone getting your pension, it will be increased by one seventh of a penny for each £1.00 of its weekly rate at the time you do eventually claim it. Broadly speaking, this means that you'll increase the value of your pension by about an extra seven and a half per cent if you postpone it for a year. There is, however, no corresponding increase for dependants.

Q: What happens if I continue to work for an employer after postponing my pension?

A: You will no longer have to pay your share of NI contributions, although your employer will continue to pay theirs. And, if you're self-employed, you will no longer have to pay Class 2 NI contributions. Neither will you have to pay Class 4 contributions for any tax year after the one in which you reach pensionable age, but you may still have to pay these during the first year of retirement.

Q: How do married women qualify for a pension?

A: Married women can qualify in one of two ways: 1) either because of your own NI contributions; or 2) you can qualify for a Basic Pension based on your husband's NI record if he is getting a pension and you are over the age of 60. Additionally, you may also be entitled to Additional Pension on the same basis as a man or a single woman.

Q: What's the situation with regard to widows?

A: It depends upon your age when you were widowed. If this happened before you reached age 60, you will have three choices open to you: 1) you can claim a Retirement Pension; or 2) continue to receive any Widow's Benefit to which you are entitled until you do wish to claim your pension or reach the age of 65; 3) postpone getting your Retirement Pension, carry on working and give up any Widow's Benefit you may be getting; this will enable you to earn extra increments for when you eventually claim your pension. And, whichever you choose, you are allowed to change your mind any time before you're 65.

If you were widowed after the age of 60, you will generally get a Retirement Pension based on your late husband's contributions. You may also be entitled to Widow's Benefit. If so, you may get a Widow's Payment but a Retirement Pension will usually be paid instead of any Widow's Pension or Widowed Mother's Allowance to which you may be entitled.
The situation for widowers is somewhat different:
If you're widowed before age 65 and not entitled to a full Basic Pension, your late wife's NI record may be taken into account to increase your pension. And, if you were incapable of work when your wife died or became so within 13 weeks of being widowed, you may be able to claim Invalidity Pension on your late wife's NI record.

In the case of a man widowed after age 65, there are two possibilities: 1) if you're not entitled to a full Basic Pension and your wife was under 60 when she died, her NI record may be taken into account to increase your pension entitlement. But, if your wife was over 60, you may be able to get a Retirement Pension based on her NI record plus one based on both your own and her NI records up to the maximum a single person can get.

Q: What about people who have divorced?

A: If you're not entitled to a full Basic Pension, your former spouse's NI record may be taken into account if this will give you a better pension. However, this is only providing you have not remarried before reaching pension age. You don't have to wait until your former spouse is getting his or her pension before applying for yours.

16 How To Get Well-Paid Government Jobs

A job might not be considered as a 'benefit' in the strictest sense of the word. None the less, it certainly can be of great benefit to the job holder and this chapter will give you an insight into how to go about becoming a Government employee.

In times of general economic difficulty, there is a lot to be said for working for the Government. First of all, the chances of being made redundant are generally smaller than for industry and commerce in general. Secondly, even when the economy as a whole may be contracting, this contraction in itself can often lead to the creation of more Government jobs.

For example, the Department of Social Security – which is charged with the administration of so many of the benefits listed elsewhere in this book – is increasing its manpower. The planned number of 'man-years', which is not quite the same thing as number of employees, but near enough for comparison purposes, for the DSS in 1993-94 was 87,550; and it has been estimated that this will rise to 88,359 in 1994-95. Here's a clear-cut example of how even a national economy which at best may be described as stagnant may still lead to an increase in the number of Government jobs in one department.

The Government, through its various departments and agencies, employs people in all sorts of capacities to do just about any kind of work. In fact, you'd be hard put to come up with a type of job that doesn't exist in one form or another within Government. Typists, accountants, foresters, surveyors, statisticians, you name it, members of almost any kind of occupation, trade or profession, are employed by one Government department or another.

Until not so long ago, recruitment for Government jobs was the exclusive preserve of a central body – the Civil Service Commission, which incorporated the Civil Service Selection Board – but this has changed considerably over the years. Just over ten years ago the responsibility for recruitment to junior grades (that is below Executive Officer level) was transferred to the individual departments. An even greater change took place in 1991 when, by Order in Council, the responsibility for recruitment below grade 7 (what used to be known as the 'Principal' grade) was also given over to individual departments and executive agencies. What this meant was that, in effect, each department was left to 'do its own thing' as far as recruiting staff was concerned.

Although free to follow their own recruitment policies – except for the very top jobs – the departments none the less are expected to obey a 'Good Practice in Recruitment' code which is recommended by the Civil Service Commissioners.

And, one of the key points of that code is concerned with 'fair and open competition', when it states that vacancies below Executive Officer level should be publicised at least in the local Jobcentre; and by advertisement in the local, national or specialist press for middle and senior appointments.

As far as can be ascertained, the code is adhered to by departments in varying degrees with a 'fair number of vacancies actually being notified to Jobcentres. However, it does mean that the job seeker may have to contact several Jobcentres to find out what vacancies there are within a reasonable travelling distance because a job may only be notified to the local Jobcentre and therefore they may not get to hear of the one just a few miles further down the road.

Jobcentres are aware of this problem and applicants may ask them to check with other Jobcentres in the region to find out whether there are any Government vacancies. Whether this in fact will be done and how far the search may be extended will vary somewhat from Jobcentre to Jobcentre. There is nothing, of course, to stop you from contacting other Jobcentres yourself.

Jobcentres remain the best source of information about vacancies for most lower grade jobs, but middle level jobs will generally be advertised in either national newspapers or specialist publications, although they should still be notified to the Department of Employment.

Now that each Government department is pursuing its own recruitment policy, what really happens in terms of notifying local Jobcentres will vary considerably. Here, to give you an idea of how great that variation can be, are some comments from various departments.

The Forestry Commission: "It is part of our policy to notify the local Jobcentre of a specific vacancy. In our letter we ask the Jobcentre to advise their other offices of the vacancy."

Central Statistical Office: "Vacancies for generalist staff are usually advertised, eg through the national press or through Jobcentres ... vacancies at Administrative Officer level and below are generally notified at Jobcentres."

HMSO: "Vacancies are generally advertised, some of which being notified to Jobcentres."

Office of Fair Trading: "Vacancies are, if necessary, advertised externally by means of the press and/or placing our vacancies in Jobcentres."

From this small sample, you can see that you can't always rely upon your Jobcentre necessarily knowing about any suitable Government job, although they will probably have details of most of them. In fact, there is no way that you can be sure of getting to know of all the vacancies because contacting the various departments directly will not always do the trick either, as they have varying policies on how to deal with enquiries which are not for specific vacancies.

However, there is a three point plan that you can follow to be certain of getting to know of as many vacancies as reasonably possible:

1) Contact your local Jobcentre and explain your interest in getting a Government job and ask to be told of any current or future vacancies. Also ask your Jobcentre to check with other Jobcentres in your area.

2) Check with other Jobcentres in your area yourself.

3) Write directly to the Personnel Department of the Government department which is likely to have the kind of job you're after. This may result in you receiving details of specific vacancies although that might not be so. They will, however, generally send you an information pack which will usually contain details of the kind of jobs they have, the conditions, the qualifications needed, and where their jobs are advertised. When you write, ask if they would please let you know of suitable vacancies when they arise. It obviously helps if you can indicate what kind of job you're looking for. You'll find a list of the addresses of major Government departments and agencies at the end of **Chapter 18 – How to Get Valuable Free Information**.

LOCAL GOVERNMENT JOBS

If the road to finding a Government job may be complicated, this can become even more so when trying to find work in local Government, as each authority is very much its own master and the procedures may vary substantially.

Once again, most jobs up to a certain level will usually be notified to local Jobcentres and there is a greater likelihood that any vacancies will be advertised in your local newspapers. However, this is not always the case and specialist jobs may only be advertised in certain national papers or the specialist press.

But there is a way that you can get to know of many more local Government jobs above a certain level and that is by getting a publication called *Opportunities – the public sector recruitment weekly* which lists vacancies from all over the country. You can get this paper on subscription by writing to: *Opportunities, Link House, West Street, Poole, Dorset BH15 1LL* at a cost of £10 for 12 issues. But, if you happen to know someone who is working in local Government, you can possibly get it free of charge by asking your acquaintance to pick it up at work for you as the paper is distributed free of charge to every department of every Local Authority in the country.

A brief sample of the kind of vacancies advertised in one issue of Opportunities included: Town Clerk (Bath), Office Manager (Islington), Pest Control Operative (Reading), Repairs Officers (Hammersmith and Fulham), Typing Pool Supervisor (Hackney), Recreation Supervisor (South Derbyshire), Engineer (Bromley) and so on.

17 Other Sources Of Help And Advice

There are many organisations whose activities dovetail and overlap with those of the Government departments described in previous chapters. Most of these are voluntary bodies, some of which may be partially funded by Government. Although there are literally hundreds of such groups, the ones listed hereafter were chosen for inclusion because their areas of interest are closely linked with the benefits described in other parts of this book.

Age Concern, Astral House, 1268 London Road, London SW16 4ER (081-679 8000), is a campaigning pressure group that works on behalf of the elderly. It also publishes various fact sheets – including Help with Heating, Raising Income or Capital from Your Home, Dental Care in Retirement, Income Tax and Older People, Help with Telephones, Older Home Owners: Financial Help with Repairs, Your State Pension and Carrying on Working – which are available free on receipt of a 9" x 6" SAE.

British Association for Counselling, 1 Regent Place, Rugby CV21 2PJ (0788-578 328). Members of this association are individuals and organisations concerned with counselling in a variety of settings. The Information Office publishes directories listing counselling services. Please send an SAE with enquiries.

British Rail produce two free leaflets, British Rail and Disabled Travellers, a general guide to special facilities, and Disabled Persons Railcard, which you can get from your local station.

Care and Repair is the national name of local schemes that help elderly home-owners improve and repair their homes so that they can continue to live there in comfort and security. The advisory services provided by Care and Repair are absolutely free and they will seek out sources of grants on behalf of their clients and will often be able to have the work done at either no cost, or a nominal one, to the occupier. You can find out whether there is a Care and Repair scheme in your area by contacting your local authority or you can find out from the national co-ordinating body at: *Care and Repair, Castle House, Kirtley Drive, Nottingham NG7 1LD (0602-799 091).* Alternatively find out if there is a similar scheme in your area known as Staying Put, which is often run by a housing association, which does broadly similar work.

Carers' National Association, 20/25 Glasshouse Yard, London EC1A 4JS (071-490 8818), offers support and information to people caring for relatives and friends and can put carers in touch with local sources of help. Offers a wide range of free leaflets.

Citizens' Advice Bureaux. Partially funded by a grant from the Department of Trade and Industry, the National Association of Citizens' Advice Bureaux consists of more than 1,300 outlets which offer free and impartial advice on all kinds of matters, including debts, homelessness, equal opportunities, employment, education and training, welfare rights, immigration and Social Security. You'll find a CAB in just about every city and town. To locate your nearest bureau, look in your telephone directory under Citizens' Advice Bureaux.

Criminal Injuries Compensation Board, Tay House, 300 Bath Street, Glasgow G2 4JR (041-331 2726), was set up in 1964 to compensate victims of 'crimes of violence and its funding comes from the Home Office and the Scottish Office. Compensation is in the main paid for pain and suffering, but the Board also takes into account loss of wages caused by the injury. Fatal injuries applications are also received from the dependants and the relatives of victims who have died as a result of their injuries. Since its inception, the Board has dealt with more than 730,420 applications up to the end of March 1993. In 1992/93 they dealt with 65,977 cases for which the total compensation paid out was £152,201,131. They produce an excellent Guide to the Criminal Injuries Compensation Scheme which you can get from them and also usually from local Citizens' Advice Bureaux. Major changes are likely to be introduced in the near future into how compensation is calculated with the new system proposed being based on a 'tariff' scale instead of by the more complicated assessment method being used currently. It is expected that the proposed changes – which will be introduced by ministerial order rather than by Parliamentary vote – will mean that four out of ten claimants will receive less.

Cruse – Bereavement Care, Cruse House, 126 Sheen Road, Richmond, Surrey TW9 1UR (081-940 4818), offers help to all bereaved people through its local branches which also run courses for volunteer counsellors. They also publish various leaflets and books on what to do after a death, living through loss, depression, etc, and you can get a list of these by sending them an SAE.

Disabled Living Foundation, 380-384 Harrow Road, London W9 2HV, provides advice on all aspects of daily living for disabled people.

The Family Fund, PO Box 50, York, YO1 2ZX, is a Government fund independently run by the Joseph Rowntree Foundation to help families who are caring for a child who is very severely handicapped by a disability. There is no formal means test for this help, but the Fund says "we can only help with modest needs related to the care of the child. Families with a good income could usually afford many of the things for which we give grants." Help from the Fund has included such things as a washing machine because the child's disability causes constant bedwetting, holidays and outings to relieve stress, driving lessons for the main carer of the child. Generally help is only available until the child reaches the age of 16. They also publish a variety of free leaflets, including a benefits checklist.

Family Welfare Association, 501-505 Kingsland Road, London E8 4AU (071-254 6251), "...administers a wide variety of trust funds from which we make grants to people in need living in all parts of the UK. The applications must be made by Social Workers on behalf of a client and the decisions are made by a voluntary committee of people with a wide variety of expertise, mostly within the social work field." The Association also runs *EGAS – Educational Grants Advisory Service* – which advises students on appropriate educational trusts to which they can apply for extra help and also advises on mandatory and discretionary grants and other possible sources of finance.

Gingerbread, 35 Wellington Street, London WC2E 7BN (071-240 0953), is a network of local self-help groups for single parents, and a national advice line for one-parent families.

Help the Aged, St James's Walk, London EC1R 0BE (071-253 0253), offers help, advice and information, and campaigns on behalf of the aged.

The Marine Society, 202 Lambeth Road, London SE1 7JW (071-261 9535), produces a free leaflet that lists no less than 39 charities that provide help for seafarers and their dependants.

MAVIS – Mobility Advice and Vehicle Information Service, TRRL, Crowthorne, Berkshire RG11 6AU (0344-773 131), is part of the Department of Transport and gives advice on car adaptations for disabled drivers and passengers.

MIND – National Association for Mental Health, Granta House, 15/19 Broadway, London E15 4BQ (081-519 2122), provides advice and information for carers of people with any form of mental illness. There are local branches in most parts of the country.

National Society for the Prevention of Cruelty to Children (NSPCC), produces a variety of useful publications which are available free of charge from: *NSPCC National Centre Library, 42 Curtain Road, London EC2A 3NH (071-825 2500).* Titles include:

Sad Children, Happy Children; Speaking out about Child Abuse ... what every young person should know; Why you should ring the NSPCC; Child abuse investigations: a guide for children and young people; Child protection procedures: a guide for adults.

Motability, Gate House, 2nd Floor, West Gate, The High, Harlow, Essex CM20 1HR, is an independent charity that helps disabled people who are getting Mobility Allowance or war pensioner's Mobility Supplement to hire new cars or to buy on HP new cars, used cars and powered wheelchairs on preferential terms.

National Association of Councils for Voluntary Service (NACVS), *3rd Floor, Arundel Court, 117 Arundel Street, Sheffield S1 2NU (0742-786 636),* is a central body that provides information about local Councils for Voluntary Service.

National Association of Widows, *54-57 Allison Street, Digbeth, Birmingham B5 5TH (021-643 8348),* offers advice and support to widows.

National Council for One-Parent Families, *255 Kentish Town Road, London NW5 2LX (071-267 1361),* describes itself as being "at the forefront of training, information and campaigning services for lone parents". It offers specialist advice to one-parent families on financial matters, housing problems, legal rights and associated problems. It also produces a wide range of booklets and leaflets.

Neighbourhood Energy Action, *2-4 Bigg Market, Newcastle-upon-Tyne NE1 1UW,* is a national charity which promotes practical help and advice on home insulation and energy use for people on low income.

Parentline *(Organisations for Parents under Stress), Westbury House, 57 Hart Road, Thundersley, Essex SS7 3PD (0268-757 077)* runs a network of telephone helplines for parents under stress.

The Parent Network, *44-46 Caversham Road, London NW5 2DS (071-485 8535),* is the central organisation for local groups that offer support and ideas on how to handle the ups and downs of family life.

Police Complaints Authority, *10 Great George Street, London SW1P 3AE,* is an independent public watchdog body that will supervise the investigation of serious complaints against police officers. Its purpose is to see that whenever a complaint is made about the conduct of a police officer it is dealt with thoroughly and, above all, fairly.

RADAR – The Royal Association for Disability and Rehabilitation, *15 Mortimer Street, London W1N 8AB,* can arrange for discounts on new cars for the disabled. Their Scottish address is: *Disability*

Scotland, Princes House, 5 Shandwick Place, Edinburgh EH2 4RG.

Relate – National Marriage Guidance, Herbert Gray College, Little Church Street, Rugby, Warwickshire CV21 3AP (0788-573 241), has local organisations throughout the country that offer relationship counselling.

Royal National Institute for the Blind, 224 Great Portland Street, London W1N 6AA (071-388 1266).

Royal National Institute for the Deaf, 105 Gower Street, London WC1E 6AH (071-387 8033).

The Salvation Army, 101 Queen Victoria Street, London EC4P 4EP, through its branches nationwide provides all kinds of help, including in an average year 85,000 food parcels, 250,000 articles of clothing and nearly 50,000 items of furniture to needy people. It also provides 2,500 beds for the homeless every night and, at any one time, a further 1,600 people are living in their resettlement programmes.

Samaritans. A voluntary organisation with 171 branches throughout the country that offer confidential emotional support 24 hours a day. You'll find your local branch listed in your phone book.

The Soldiers', Sailors' and Airmen's Families Association and the Forces Help Society, 19 Queen Elizabeth Street, London SE1 2LP (071-403 8783), "exists to serve the families of all men and women who serve, or have served, in the Armed Services, the Reserves or the Territorial Army", and their representatives will, among other things, negotiate with gas and electricity authorities, housing departments, HP firms, regarding debts due to unemployment, illness or disability; apply to charities when financial help is needed; provide emergency grants to meet urgent requirements; organise long-term counselling for families with special problems; visit widows, old and young, giving financial advice and keeping an eye on their welfare.

The Women's Royal Voluntary Service (WRVS), provides a wide range of caring services for the elderly and families in need throughout the UK. Your nearest local office will be listed in your phone book.

18 How To Get Valuable Free Information

Apart from the various grants and benefits outlined in previous chapters, the Government is also a unique source of another very valuable commodity – free information on just about every subject imaginable.

This information is, of course, primarily collected by Government to enable it to run its own business, but a great deal of it has been assembled in easy-to-read leaflets and booklets, many of which are yours free for the asking.

The amount of this information is so vast – the publications catalogue of just one Government department has more than 1,700 separate items – that it would be beyond the scope of this book to list it all. However, in the rest of this chapter, you will find a sampling of the sort of things that are available and at the end you will find out how you can get free information from the Government on the subjects that particularly interest you.

All the material mentioned specifically is free of charge, but there are also many more items that are available at modest cost.

Department of Social Security. The Benefits Agency of this Department produces an excellent catalogue of Benefits Agency, Social Security and Contributions Agency leaflets, booklets and posters. In the hundreds of items listed, you will find all the DSS literature mentioned elsewhere in this book. You can get the catalogue itself (*ref: CAT1*) and all the items listed in it (apart from a few exceptions) from: *BA Publications, Heywood Stores, Manchester Road, Heywood, Lancashire OL10 2PZ*. Orders can also be faxed through on *0706-622 955*.

Department of Health. All the leaflets listed in Chapter 7 of this book, How to Collect Free Prescriptions and Other Health Benefits, can be obtained, apart from the sources mentioned in the text, from: *BAPS, Storage and Distribution Centre, Health Publications Unit, Heywood Stores, Manchester Road, Heywood, Lancashire OL10 2PZ*. On a different matter, you can also get free from this address two excellent publications: Drugs – A Parent's Guide: the signs, the dangers, what to do; and Solvents – A Parent's Guide.

Her Majesty's Stationery Office produces a vast quantity of books of all kinds for sale. Their catalogues and brochures are, however, free and you can get them by writing to: *HMSO Publicity,*

147

Department B, Freepost, Norwich NR3 1BR. Subject areas for which free catalogues or brochures are available include: Agriculture, Books for all Seasons (popular titles), Building, Business Books, Education, Environment, Food and Nutrition, Forestry, Geology, Health and Safety, History, Archaeology and Architecture, Institute of Terrestrial Ecology, Law, Medicine and Health, Military, Plants and Gardens, Social Issues.

The Department of the Environment has free publications on a wide range of environmental topics, including many beautifully produced broadsheet posters. Included are: River Quality poster; One World poster, which covers global environment issues including tropical rain forest depletion, Antarctica and climate changes; Pollution Control Systems; Global Atmosphere and Air Quality poster; Cleaner Seas poster; Countryside poster; Heritage poster; Waste and Recycling booklet; Polar Regions poster; Global Climate Changes booklet, a layman's guide to the climate and the greenhouse effect; The Ozone Layer booklet which includes up-to-date information such as satellite data from over the Antarctica; Green Rights and Responsibilities, a citizen's guide; Protected Bats postcard, a full colour postcard of the lesser horseshoe bat; Wake Up to What You Can Do for the Environment, practical tips and facts about simple actions we can all take to protect the environment. These are all available from: *Department of the Environment, PO Box 135, Bradford, West Yorshire BD9 4HU.*

Additionally, the Department of the Environment publishes a wide range of free booklets on housing matters and you should be able to get these from your local authority. Titles include: The Tenant's Charter; Right to Repair; Assured Tenancies; Letting Rooms in Your Home; Regulated Tenancies; A Guide for Tenants of Housing Associations; Your Right to Buy Your Home; Tenants' Choice; Repairs; He Wants Me Out; The Rights and Duties of Landlords and Tenants of Houses; Paying for Repairs and Improvements to your Home; A Householder's Planning Guide for the Installation of Satellite Television Dishes; Planning: A Householder's Guide.

The Office of Fair Trading produces a range of free consumer advice publications; here's just a few: Square Deal, consumer topics; Dear Shopper in Scotland, Dear Shopper in Northern Ireland, explaining the differences in legal and advisory procedures in different parts of the UK; Bon Voyage, advice on holidays and what to do if things go wrong; How To Cope with Doorstep Salesmen; Buying by Post; Home Improvements; Shoes; Used Cars – a Guide for People Who Know Little About Them; Moneyfax 2, a crucial guide to credit and debt; CreditWise – your guide to trouble free credit; No Credit? explains your right to know what credit agencies say about you; Debt – a survival guide, a six-step action plan to help cope with debt, including a personal budget chart and an outline financial statement for creditors; Misleading Advertisements. Order the above from: *Office of Fair Trading, Room 306, Field House, 15-25 Bream's Buildings, London EC4A 1PR.*

The Employment Department produces a series of extremely well-researched and presented booklets intended to help those running small businesses or people wishing to start up in business. Titles include: Starting and Running Your Own Business, Accounting for a Small Firm, Selling to Larger Firms, Franchising, How to Start Exporting, Tendering for Government Contracts, Trade Credit, Marketing, Your Guide to Help for Small Firms, The Secret of Business Success. All are free and you should be able to get these from your local Training and Enterprise Council or Jobcentre.

The Patent Office produces a wide range of free literature. Included are: What is intellectual property?, a pack containing basic facts about patents, copyrights, registered trade marks and service marks, and designs; Patent Protection; How to Prepare a UK Patent Application; Design Registration; Registering a Trade or Service Mark; Patent Search Services; and An Introduction to the Services of the Patent Office and Trade Marks and Designs Registries. Order these from: *The Patent Office, Marketing, Information and Publicity, Cardiff Road, Newport, Gwent NP9 1RH.*

The Forestry Commission publishes many interesting booklets and leaflets and you can get a catalogue of these from them by writing to: *Forestry Commission, Public Information Division, 231 Corstorphine Road, Edinburgh EH12 7AT.* Two free items are worth a particular mention: Forest Life, a beautifully produced all colour magazine; and an information pack filled with colour brochures about Forest Holidays.

FREE PUBLICATIONS

Here are some more free publications:

A Guide to Bankruptcy Law – from: *DTI, Insolvency Service, Bridge Place, 88-89 Eccleston Square, London SW1V 1PT.*

How to Become a Radio Amateur – from: *DTI, Radiocommunications Agency, Information and Library Service, Room 605,*

Waterloo Bridge House, Waterloo Road, London SE1 8UA.

BNSC Space News – published three times a year and available from: *British National Space Centre, Information Office, Dean Bradley House, Horseferry Road, London SW1P 2AG.*

Handy Hints to Save Energy in your Home; and Landlords: A Guide to Energy Efficiency. Both available from *Department of Energy, Distribution Centre, Blackhorse Road, London SE99 6TT.*

The publications listed above only begin to skim the surface of the vast amount of information that you can get free of charge courtesy of the Government. Strangely enough, although there are some departmental catalogues, there is no central listing and there is no way you can find out at a central point what is available.

However, if you are interested in a particular subject and wonder if there is a free Government publication about it, you can take the simple step of writing to the Department or Agency most likely to have something and ask them. Address your letter to the 'Chief Information Officer' and specify as clearly as possible what kind of information you're seeking. It would also be to your advantage when making your request to enclose an SAE.

NAMES AND ADDRESSES

Here, to help you, is a list of names and addresses:

Ministry of Agriculture, Fisheries and Food, *Whitehall Place, London SW1A 2HH (071-270 3000).*

Bank of England, *Threadneedle Street, London EC2R 8AH (071-601 4444).*

Central Office of Information, *Hercules Road, London SE1 7DU (071-928 2345).*

Central Statistical Offices, *Government Offices, Great George Street, London SW1P 3AQ (071-270 3000).*

HM Customs & Excise, *New King's Beam House, 22 Upper Ground, London SE1 9PJ (071-620 1313).*

Ministry of Defence, *Main Building, Whitehall, London SW1A 2HB (071-218 9000).*

Department for Education, *Sanctuary Building, Great Smith Street, Westminster, London SW1P 3BT (071-925 5000).*

Department of Employment, *Caxton House, Tothill Street, London SW1H 9NF (071-273 3000).*

Department of Energy, *1 Palace Street, London SW1E 5HE (071-238 3000).*

Department of the Environment, *2 Marsham Street, London SW1P 3EB (071-276 3000)*.

Foreign and Commonwealth Office, *Downing Street (West), London SW1A 2AL (071-270 3100)*.

Health and Safety Executive, *St Hugh's House, Stanley Precinct, Bootle L20 3QY (051-951 4000)*.

Department of Health, *Richmond House, 79 Whitehall, London SW1A 2NS (071-210 3000)*.

Health Education Authority, *Hamilton House, Mabledon Place, London WC1H 9TX (071-383 3833)*.

Home Office, *Queen Anne's Gate, London SW1H 9AT (071-273 3000)*.

Inland Revenue, *Cabinet Office, Great George Street, London SW1P 3AE (071-270 3000)*.

Department for National Savings, *Charles House, 375 Kensington High Street, London W14 8SD (071-605 9300)*.

Overseas Development Administration, *94 Victoria Street, London SW1E 5JL (071-917 7000)*.

The Post Office, *Post Office Headquarters, 148 Old Street, London EC1V 9HQ (071-490 2888)*.

Royal Mint, *Llantrisant, Pontyclun, Mid-Glamorgan CF7 8YT (0443-222 111)*.

The Scottish Office, *New St Andrew's House, Edinburgh EH1 3TD (031-244 1111)*.

Department of Social Security, *Richmond House, 79 Whitehall, London SW1A 2NS (071-210 3000)*.

Department of Trade and Industry, *Ashdown House, 123 Victoria Street, London SW1E 6RB (071-215 5000)*.

Department of Transport, *2 Marsham Street, London SW1P 3EB (071-276 0888)*.

HM Treasury, *Treasury Chambers, Parliament Street, London SW1P 3AG (071-270 5238)*.

Welsh Office, *Cathays Park, Cardiff CF1 3NQ (0222-825 111)*.

19 How To Collect Benefits Abroad

There are a number of Social Security benefits that you can continue to claim and receive if you leave this country. Some you can get even if you move permanently; others will only be available under special circumstances or for restricted periods of time.

The rules governing the payment of benefits to people living abroad are very complex and what you may be able to collect will often be affected by which foreign country you go to or settle in, so it's always best to check what your entitlement will be before you leave. However, we list below the main points about benefits which may continue to be available if you move abroad.

RETIREMENT PENSIONS

This is a fairly simple one because you can generally get your Retirement Pension anywhere abroad.

If you're going away for three months or less, you can normally allow your pension to build up and cash in the orders upon your return. However, bear in mind that a pension order can only be cashed in within three months of the date which is shown on it.

If you're going away for four, five or six months and you are currently being paid by automated credit transfer this method of payment can continue, allowing you to make your own arrangements for transferring your Retirement Pension or Widow's Benefit abroad. If you are being paid by order book, when all the orders up to the date of your departure have been cashed, return your order book to your nearest DSS office.

If you're going abroad for more than six months – or permanently – inform your local Social Security office in plenty of time before you leave so that they can make arrangements to get your pension paid to you abroad.

If you're living abroad when pension rates are increased in the UK, you may be able to get the increased rate only if: 1) you are living in a European Community (EC) country, including Gibraltar; or 2) you are living in a country with which the UK has a reciprocal agreement which permits you to receive the increased rate – these countries are: Austria, Barbados, Bermuda, Cyprus, Finland, Iceland, Israel, Jamaica, Jersey, Guernsey and Alderney, Malta, Mauritius,

Norway, Phillipines, Sweden, Switzerland, Turkey, USA.

WIDOW'S BENEFITS

Broadly, the same rules apply as for Retirement Pensions (see above). But dependency increases for a child will only be paid: 1) if you're not going to stay abroad; or 2) if you go to live in an EC country and do not get a pension from that country; or 3) if you go to live in a country where a reciprocal agreement provides for an increase for a child (see list above).

As far as increases that take place in the rate while you're abroad, the rules are the same as for Retirement Pensions.

CHILD BENEFIT AND ONE-PARENT BENEFIT

You can usually continue to get these for the first eight weeks of a temporary absence abroad.

However, if you are going abroad for longer than eight weeks, your benefit will stop from the date of departure. But in many countries you will be able to get the social security benefits of those countries. What you should do is get *leaflet CH6 – Child Benefit for People Leaving Britain* from the DSS, complete the form at the back of it and send it to your local DSS office with your order book, if you have one.

What you may receive while living permanently abroad will vary considerably, as Great Britain has reciprocal Social Security agreements with many other countries. These agreements may either allow you to qualify earlier for those countries' child benefit or may help you to continue getting the benefits you received while you were living here. You'll find fuller details in the leaflet referred to above.

There are special rules concerning women who leave here temporarily and have a baby within eight weeks of leaving. Child Benefit is likely to be paid from the date of birth until the end of the eight week period.

FAMILY CREDIT

If you are already getting Family Credit when you go abroad, you will continue to be entitled for the rest of your current 26-week award period. Before you go abroad, you can make arrangements for payment by writing to: *DSS, Family Credit, Government Buildings, Warbreck Hill Road, Blackpool FY2 OAX.*

GUARDIAN'S ALLOWANCE

This will normally continue to be payable anywhere if your absence abroad, or the child's, is for less than eight weeks and as long as you can still continue to receive Child Benefit for the child.

INCOME SUPPORT

Although the purpose of Income Support is to meet the needs of people in this country, it can still be claimed abroad by some people for the first four weeks of a temporary absence abroad – or for eight weeks if they are going abroad for a dependant's medical treatment.

In order to qualify during the first four weeks, you must continue to be eligible during that period and your absence must be unlikely to be longer than a year. Additionally, you must be exempt from having to sign on as available for and actively seeking work.

You will also continue to get Income Support if: 1) you're incapable of work and the sole purpose of your absence is to receive medical treatment for that incapacity; or 2) you have a partner who is going abroad with you and for whom you get one of the three pensioner premiums or a disability premium; or 3) on the day the absence began, you had been incapable of work for at least the previous 28 weeks.

To qualify for eight weeks' payment, the absence should also be for less than a year and you, or you and a member of your family must be accompanying a dependant abroad solely for the purpose of that dependant's medical treatment by an appropriately qualified person.

Even though you may be entitled to Income Support, the payment will not be sent to you abroad and usually you will receive it upon your return here. Alternatively, payment can be made to another person, usually your partner, who has remained here.

WAR PENSIONS

Both War Pensions and War Widows' Pensions may continue to be paid anywhere abroad, although there are some for whom the arrangements may be different.

You will find more information in *leaflet MPL120 – War Pensioners and War Widows Going Abroad – Your Pension and Welfare Service*, which also has in it *form PF16R* which you should complete and post to the address given if you're going abroad for more than three months. To obtain this leaflet or for more information write to *War Pensions Agency, Norcross, Blackpool FY5 3WP*, or phone the *War Pensions Helpline on 0253-858 858*.

INVALID CARE ALLOWANCE

You may be able to continue receiving this if you are going abroad temporarily and you should send details of your planned absence well in advance of your departure to: *ICA Unit, DSS, Palatine House, Lancaster Road, Preston PR1 1HB*.

SEVERE DISABLEMENT ALLOWANCE

Generally, you will not be able to get this when you're out of the UK, but you may be able to do so if your absence is just for a temporary visit or you are going to an EC country. Contact your local DSS office well in advance of your journey.

STATUTORY SICK PAY

You will be able to get this if you are working for an employer or on holiday from your employment in a country which is a member of the European Economic Area (EEA). The EEA includes the countries in the European Community and also Austria, Finland, Iceland, Norway and Sweden.

If you are working for a UK employer outside the EEA, Statutory

Sick Pay will not be paid but you may be able to claim Sickness Benefit instead.

INDUSTRIAL INJURIES BENEFITS

If you are getting one of these benefits before you go abroad, you can continue getting it after you leave, subject to the conditions below:

Disablement Pensions and Industrial Death Benefit can generally be paid anywhere abroad at the full rate.

Constant Attendance Allowance is usually paid for the first six months of a temporary absence, but this period may be extended.

Reduced Earnings Allowance and Unemployability Supplement can usually be paid for the first three months of your absence, but also sometimes for longer, provided that you started getting the allowance before you left and have not gone abroad to work. Special provisions may apply if you are going to an EC country or to one with which the UK has a two-way agreement.

UNEMPLOYMENT BENEFIT

You cannot get Unemployment Benefit abroad. However, if you're going to another country within the EC to look for work, you may be able to get benefit in that country. For more information get *booklet UBL22 Unemployment Benefit for People Going Abroad* from your Jobcentre.

SICKNESS AND INVALIDITY BENEFITS AND MATERNITY ALLOWANCE

To receive these you must have gone abroad only temporarily and one of the two following conditions must apply: 1) you went abroad for the specific purpose of receiving treatment for an incapacity that began before you left here; or 2) you must have been continuously incapable of work for at least six months up to the time you left. Once again, special provisions may apply if you are going to an EC country or one with which the UK has a two-way agreement.

FOR ADDITIONAL INFORMATION

If you're going to an EC country (including Gibraltar) or a country which is a member of the European Free Trade Association (Australia, Finland, Ireland, Norway and Sweden), you should get *leaflet SA29 – Your Social Security Insurance, Benefits and Health Care Rights in the European Community* from: *DSS, Overseas Benefits Directorate, Newcastle-upon-Tyne NE98 1YX.*

As far as countries outside the EC are concerned, the UK has two-way agreements with a number of these and you can get a leaflet that explains the particular agreement for each of those countries from the DSS at the address directly above. The countries covered by the leaflets are: Australia (leaflet number *SA4*), Austria (*SA25*), Barbados (*SA43*), Bermuda (*SA23*), Canada (*SA20*), Cyprus (*SA12*), Finland (*SA19*), Iceland (*SA24*), Israel (*SA14*), Jamaica (*SA27*), Jersey and Guernsey (*SA4*), Malta (*SA11*), Mauritius (*SA38*), New Zealand (*SA8*), Norway (*SA16*), Phillipines *(SA42)*, Sweden (*SA9*), Switzerland (*SA6*), Turkey (*SA22*) and USA (*SA33*).

SERVICE FAMILIES WORKING ABROAD

The rules for members of the Armed Forces serving abroad and their families are quite different in many respects.

First of all, although serving members of the forces, whether in the UK or abroad, have Class 1 National Insurance contributions taken from their pay, these are at a lower rate than those paid by civilians because Armed Forces personnel do not have the same rights to benefits. On the other hand, they do have certain special schemes of their own run by the Ministry of Defence. Although full details of these schemes are outside the scope of this book, here is a brief mention of some of them:

Family Credit. Service personnel abroad should ask at their pay unit about claiming this benefit under the MoD scheme.

Income Support. This benefit is not usually available because one of its conditions is that you or your partner must not be working more than 16 hours a week. In the case of a wife in the UK who is claiming Income Support on the grounds that she is separated from her husband, the Child Support Agency will usually ask the husband to pay maintenance even if he is abroad.

Housing Benefit. The MoD run their own benefit scheme to provide assistance to those who need help to pay their Crown

Tenancy rent. This is available to families living in MoD accommodation either in the UK or abroad.

For more information. Get *leaflet FB5 – Service Families Going Abroad* from your local DSS office or from your BFPO or HIVE.

Appendices

Many benefits share common rules as part of the conditions which determine eligibility. These are listed below and cross references to these appendices have been inserted in the main text of this book where relevant.

APPENDIX A

COMMON RULES FOR INCOME SUPPORT, HOUSING BENEFIT, COUNCIL TAX BENEFIT, DISABILITY WORKING ALLOWANCE AND FAMILY CREDIT.

CAPITAL RULES

The Upper Limit (if you have more than this in savings, you won't qualify for the benefit):

There are two different Upper Limits – the lowest of these is £8,000 and applies to Family Credit and Income Support. For the other benefits listed above it is £16,000.

Of these amounts (and this applies to all the listed benefits), savings of £3,000 or less will be completely ignored in the calculation of entitlement. Savings between £3,000 and the relevant Upper Limit will affect the amount of benefit you get as £1.00 a week will be taken into account for every £250 or part of £250 when entitlement is assessed. The DSS, however, stresses that this is not intended to represent any particular rate of return from capital invested and that the formula is not linked in any way to interest rates and therefore does not alter in line with any changes in these rates. Here's how it works in practice:

Example 1. If your savings are £6,256, £14 a week is taken into account in calculating entitlement.

Example 2. In the case of savings of £4,025, £5 a week is taken into account.

It is also worth looking at what the DSS considers as capital as certain rather important possessions are completely ignored for this purpose. These include most personal possessions and, most importantly, your home. Other property owned by you will usually be counted as capital, but there are exceptions, so if you own more than one home check with the Benefits Agency or your local council if you are claiming Housing Benefit or Council Tax Benefit.

Generally, however, all the money you have in whatever form it might be, such as cash, bank and building society accounts, investment trusts, shares, etc, is counted as capital when entitlement to benefit is assessed. And, the source of such money makes no difference either – whether it came from savings, inheritance, redundancy payments or lump-sum grants. There are, as only to be expected, some exceptions and these include sums that had to be deposited with a Housing Association as part of your tenancy or capital that is 'earmarked' for certain specific purposes. Examples of earmarked capital are the money coming from the sale of a house that is expected to be used for home purchase, compensation for a burglary or loss or damage to a house, and certain capital set aside for essential repairs or improvements. Usually, this earmarked capital is ignored for up to six months, and possibly longer under certain circumstances.

INCOME (except for Housing Benefit and Council Tax Benefit, for which see further below)

These are just some of the things that are counted as 'earnings' or 'other income' and make up what the DSS considers to be your income: remuneration or profit from employment, wages or salary, fees, commission, bonuses, tips, gratuities, most holiday pay, expenses paid by an employer which are not the direct result of your work (for example child-minding costs or the expenses of getting to work), Statutory Sick Pay and Statutory Maternity Pay. This list does not, however, include all the things that might be counted as earnings because in every case the Adjudication Officer will decide what specific earnings are to be included.

There is also a special way to work out what the average amount of bonuses or commission payments are. Broadly speaking, this consists of adding up all such payments for a year and then dividing by 52.

Certain earnings are 'disregarded', that is, not counted as part of your income. These 'disregards' include most earnings in kind (such as food, meals, etc), any child's or young person's earnings, earnings from employment which are paid outside the UK if the transfer of these earnings is prohibited. A certain amount of earnings from part-time employment (less than 16 hours a week) can also be disregarded. For most unemployed people, this disregard level is set at £5 a week, although members of certain groups such as lone parents and some disabled people qualify for a higher disregard of £15.

Many Social Security benefits are ignored completely (notably, Housing Benefit, Council Tax Benefit, Child Benefit, Attendance Allowance, Disability Living Allowance, the Christmas Bonus and certain others). Most of the others are taken fully into account although there is a £10 disregard for War Widow's and War Widower's Pension, War Disablement Pension or equivalent payments made by foreign Social Security schemes. It is important to note that this £10 disregard is subject to a general maximum £10 disregard on all income (other than earned income) and is not in addition to this. Income is, however, worked out somewhat differently for Housing Benefit and Council Tax Benefit. The main guidelines are:

☐ Income includes earnings, Social Security benefits, occupational or personal pensions and any other money you have coming in.

☐ A person can earn between £5 and £25 a week, depending on their circumstances, before any earnings are counted when entitlement to HB/CTB is assessed. The assessment of likely income from earnings should normally be based on an average earnings over the five weeks (if paid weekly) or two months (if paid monthly) preceding the date of the claim for HB/CTB. However, where these weeks or months are not representative of a person's normal average earnings, a local authority may assess earnings on the basis it considers will most accurately reflect likely average earnings over the benefit period. This helps to ensure that fluctuations in earnings are accurately reflected in a person's HB/CTB.

☐ Most Social Security benefits are counted as income when entitlement to HB/CTB is assessed, but Attendance Allowance and Disability Living Allowance are ignored or 'disregarded' in full. The first £10 of a War Widow's Pension or War Disablement Pension is also disregarded. A local authority may also operate a local scheme to increase the £10 disregard of War Widow's or War Disablement Pension, or make it total, when entitlement is assessed, but not all authorities operate such schemes.

Other factors that are taken into account when assessing entitlement to benefit are as follows.

EXPENSES FOR SUB-TENANTS

There are also important conditions relating to money you receive from lodgers, as the first £20 of what you get plus half of the balance is ignored. And, if you sub-let part of your home to a tenant, the first £4 a week of any payment is ignored plus an extra £8.60 if part or full heating is provided.

Other income that is usually ignored is money you get for fostering children, although some of the money you might receive as an adoption allowance or a custodian payment from a local authority or private agency will be taken into account.

SELF-EMPLOYED EARNINGS

Your income will be assessed by deducting allowable business expenses, tax, NI contributions and certain other costs from your averaged gross receipts. You will normally have to supply details of actual receipts and expenses to establish your income level.

NOTIONAL INCOME

Income that you don't actually have may be taken into account in certain special circumstances. Called 'notional' income, this ruling may be invoked if it is considered that you have deliberately deprived yourself of income to get benefits or failed to acquire income that is available to you.

APPENDIX B

LIVING TOGETHER AS HUSBAND AND WIFE

Many Social Security benefits can be affected if a couple are living together as husband and wife. In some instances, this can mean a reduced benefit and in others it results in the payment being stopped altogether. It can therefore be quite important to be aware of the circumstances under which the DSS may consider you and your partner to be living together as husband and wife.

'Partner', of course, is the current term used to denote a person of the opposite sex living with the claimant and you will find this used quite frequently in all DSS leaflets and booklets. The guidance on this terminology says that couples who live together as husband and wife are known as 'claimant' and 'partner', but that the word 'partner' should only be used when it is established that the relationship is that of a couple.

For example, how much Family Credit you may be able to get is affected not just by your financial situation but also by your partner's and it is a general rule that unmarried couples who are living together as husband and wife – the former term for this was 'cohabitation' – must be treated the same as a married couple. Other benefits that are affected if you are a couple are Income Support and Social Fund payments.

Benefits that cannot be paid at all to couples living together as husband and wife include: One-Parent Benefit (the logic behind this is obvious), Widow's Benefit, War Widow's Pension and Child's Special Allowance.

The DSS stress that anyone who is getting a benefit and is either living or starts living with someone else should inform them. They add: "If the situation is not clear from your claim form someone from your Social Security office will visit you. It will help you if both people are at home when the visit is made."

However, it is worthwhile pointing out that the person who visits you is not the one who will be making the actual decision because that is done by an Adjudication Officer, who is independent of the DSS. To reach his decision, he must take into account the various guidelines to help him decide whether you're living together as husband and wife, including:

a) *Are both partners members of the same household? And do either have any other home where they normally live?* Factors taken into account here would include whether the couple usually share meals and do jobs around the house for each other.

b) *Is the relationship an established one? Is it more than an occasional or very brief association?* However, when a couple first starts living together, it may be clear from the start that the relationship is similar to that of husband and wife. For example, the woman may take the man's name and may have borne his child.

c) *How are the couple's finances arranged?* In most husband and wife relationships it would be expected to find that one helps support the other or, that they share household expenses. However, the guidelines do also say "the absence of any such arrangement does not prove that two people are not living together as husband and wife".

d) *Is there a sexual relationship?* If there is one it would be considered an important factor in making the decision. But the absence of such a relationship would not necessarily prove that the couple are not living together as husband and wife as far as the DSS is concerned. Claimants should be aware that the DSS visitor is not entitled to ask about any sexual relationship, but that they may volunteer to give information about this if they think it will help make things clearer.

e) *Children?* Says the DSS: "When a couple are caring for a child or children of whom they are the parents, there is a strong presumption that they are living together as husband and wife."

f) *How do other people see the relationship?* Whether the couple present themselves to other people as husband and wife will be taken into account. Adds the DSS: "But many couples living together do not wish to pretend that they are actually married, and the fact that they retain their separate identities publicly as being unmarried does not mean that they cannot be regarded as living together as husband and wife."

Obviously, each case has to be judged on its merits by the Adjudication Officer, and there are many other factors which can be taken into account when deciding whether your life together with someone else is like a marriage.

APPENDIX C

EXTRA BENEFITS FOR DEPENDANTS

You may be entitled to get extra payments for dependants with various benefits. What you may be able to get will depend upon the basic benefit and whether you're claiming for a dependant adult and/or children.

DEPENDANT ADULTS

The weekly extra that you may get for a spouse or a person looking after your child varies according to the main benefit to which it is linked:
- [] With Retirement Pension on your own NI contributions, Invalidity Pension or Unemployability Supplement – £34.50.
- [] With Unemployment Benefit – £28.05, if you're under state pension age; or £34.50, if you're over pension age.
- [] With Invalid Care Allowance and Severe Disablement Allowance – £20.65.
- [] With Sickness Benefit – £33.10, if you're over state pension age; £28.05, if you're under pension age.
- [] With Maternity Allowance – £26.90.

These extra payments are, however, subject to 'additions' ...

DEPENDANT ADULT'S ADDITIONS

If your adult dependant lives with you, you will not get the extra payment if he or she earns more than the amounts listed below:
- [] With Retirement Pension, Invalidity Pension, Severe Disablement Allowance and Unemployability Supplement the standard rate is £45.45. But if your claim for extra benefits dates from before September 16th 1985, and if you are a man, the amount is instead £45.09.
- [] With Unemployment Benefit – £34.50, if you're over state pension age; or £28.05, if you're under pension age.
- [] With Invalid Care Allowance – £20.65.
- [] With Maternity Allowance – £26.90.
- [] With Sickness Benefit – £33.10, if you're over state pension age; £26.90, if you're under pension age.

Different limits apply if your dependant adult doesn't live with you:

☐ With Retirement Pension, Invalidity Pension and Unemployability Supplement – £34.50.
☐ With Severe Disablement Allowance – £20.70.

DEPENDANT CHILDREN

You may get an extra £9.80 a week for a child for whom the higher rate of Child Benefit is payable and £11.00 for each other child with the following: Retirement Pension, Widow's Benefits, Invalidity Benefit, Invalid Care Allowance, Severe Disablement Allowance, Unemployability Supplement and, if you are over pension age, with Sickness Benefit or Unemployment Benefit.

DEPENDANT CHILDREN'S ADDITIONS

The extra payment for dependant children, paid with long-term benefits, will be affected if your spouse or partner lives with you and earns more than the following limits: for the first child – £120.00; for each extra child – £16.00.

EARNINGS RULE

There are limits as to how much you may earn with certain benefits before these earnings start affecting how much you may get.

You can earn any amount while receiving Retirement Pension or a Widow's Benefit and it won't affect what you get. But if you are getting Income Support on top of either of these, any earnings might reduce your Income Support and thereby the total amount of money you receive.

Other limits are:

☐ With Invalid Care Allowance – £50.00 weekly.
☐ With Unemployment Benefit – a daily rate of £2.00; a weekly limit of £57.00.

Additionally, some people receiving Sickness Benefit or Invalidity Benefit or Severe Disablement Allowance may be allowed to earn up to £43.00 weekly if the work they're doing is of therapeutic benefit.

APPENDIX D

HOW TO APPEAL

If you think that a Social Security decision is wrong, there are ways to appeal against it. Obviously, before taking that step, it's a very good idea to contact the DSS informally and see whether matters can't be sorted out in a simpler way.

Explains the DSS: "You may think that a wrong decision has been made because some information was missing, or because a mistake was made. If so, get in touch straight away with the Social Security office or Unemployment Benefit Office that is dealing with your claim. Tell them what you think is wrong and ask them to look at your claim again. You can then request an explanation of how the decision was made."

If that explanation doesn't satisfy you and the DSS persists in what you consider to be a wrong decision, there are specific procedures for you to follow. What you need to do varies according to the type of decision it is and who made it. Here are some guidelines:

ADJUDICATION OFFICER DECISIONS

These are decisions as to whether you're entitled to benefit and, if you are, to how much. These decisions are made by Adjudicating Officers who are independent of the DSS and the Department of Employment. You have a right to appeal against almost all of these decisions to a Social Security Appeal Tribunal.

ADJUDICATING MEDICAL AUTHORITY DECISIONS

These concern things like to what extent you are disabled and are usually made by one or more doctors. You can pursue your claim before a Medical Appeal Tribunal.

ATTENDANCE ALLOWANCE BOARD DECISIONS

These are decisions about the medical questions that affect Attendance Allowance, and include such things as how much looking after a disabled person might need because of their disability. The Board can be asked to review its decision and, although it doesn't have hearings, you will be given the chance to send in extra written evidence.

SOCIAL FUND DECISIONS

Decisions dealing with Maternity Payments and Funeral Payment can be taken to a Social Security Appeal Tribunal. If you disagree with a decision about Community Care Grants, Budgeting Loans or Crisis Loans, you can ask the local Social Fund Officer to look at the decision again.

HOUSING BENEFIT AND COUNCIL TAX BENEFIT DECISIONS

These are a matter for your local authority. If you think a decision is wrong, ask how to appeal at the council office that pays the benefit.

WAR PENSIONS DECISIONS

Appeals are dealt with by special Pensions Appeals Tribunals which are set up by the Lord Chancellor's Office. You will be given information about how to appeal, and the time limit for doing so, when you receive the decision on your pension claim or on the assessment of your disablement.

There are other review and appeal procedures. For more information see DSS *booklets NI246 – How To Appeal, NI260 – A Guide to Reviews and Appeals* and *CSA2006 – Child Support Maintenance – A Guide to Reviews and Appeals.*

Finally, in many cases, if you disagree with a decision made by a Tribunal or Board, you have a further right of appeal to a Social Security Commissioner, but these appeals are limited to points of law, not on questions of fact. Neither can the Commissioner deal with medical questions, so you can't appeal if you disagree with medical findings or conclusions.

Index

Abroad, Collecting Benefits, 152-158
Access Funds, 128
Accident Line, The, 111
Additional Pension, 133
Age Addition, 134
Age Allowance, 119
Appeals, 169-170
Assistance by Way of Representation, 108
Attendance Allowance, 65
Availability for Work, 81

Basic Pension, 131-133
Beveridge, Lord, 7
Budgeting Loans, 44
Bursaries, 129
Business Success Allowance, 93-95

Career Development Loans, 90
Child Benefit, 20-21
Child Support Agency, 28-29
Christmas Bonus, 41-42
Civil Legal Aid, 108-109
Clothing Allowance, 119
Cold Weather Payments, 48-49
COMETT, 128
Comforts Allowance, 118
Common Parts Grants, 103
Common Rules, 161-164
Community Action, 86
Community Care Grants, 46
Constant Attendance Allowance, 118
Council Tax Benefit, 98-102
Criminal Legal Aid, 110-111
Crisis Loans, 45

Dental Treatment, NHS, 74
Dependants, Extra Benefits For, 167-168
Disability Living Allowance, 61-63
Disability Working Allowance, 63-64
Disabled Facilities Grants, 103-104
Duty Solicitor Scheme, 110

Education Grants And Loans, 124-129

ERASMUS, 129

Fabric Supports, NHS, 77
Family Credit, 14-19
Fixed Fee Interview, 112
Free Information, 147-151
Free Milk and Vitamins, 77-78
Freeline, 12
Funeral Costs, help with, for War Pensioners, 120-121
Funeral Payments, Social Fund, 47-48

Glasses, Vouchers for, 74-75
Government Jobs, 138-140
Graduated Pension, 133
Gratuities for Specified Minor Injuries, 117
Guardian's Allowance, 22

Health-related Benefits, 72-79
HMO Grants, 103
Home Energy Efficiency Scheme, 105
Home Responsibilities Protection, 69-70
Hospital Travel Costs, NHS, 76
House Adaptation Grants, 120
House Renovation Grants, 102-105
Housing Benefit, 98-102

Income Support, 30-36
Industrial Injuries Disablement Benefit, 66-67
Information, Free, 147-151
Invalid Care Allowance, 68-69
Invalidity Allowance, 134
Invalidity Benefit, 57-59

JIG, 85
Job Interview Guarantee (JIG), 85
Job Review Workshop, 85
Job Search Seminars, 85
Job Searcher's Allowance, 80
Job, Help in finding a, 84-87
Jobclub, 85
Jobs, Government, 138-140

Lawyers for Your Business, 111
Learning for Work, 89
Legal Advice and Assistance, 106-107
LINGUA, 129
Livewire, 97
Living together as Husband and Wife, 165-166

Loan Guarantee Scheme, 95-97
Local Government Jobs, 140-141
Local Referral Scheme, 112
Low Income Entitlement to Health Benefits, 78-79

Maternity Allowance, 25-26
Maternity Benefits, Overview, 22-23
Maternity Benefits, Upcoming changes in, 26-27
Maternity Payments, Social Fund, 47
Milk, Free, 77-78
Minor Works Assistance, 104
Mobility Supplement, 119
National Assistance Board, 8
National Health Service – see NHS
NHS Benefits, Low income entitlement, 78-79
NHS Dental Treatment, 74
NHS Hospital Travel Costs, 76
NHS Prescriptions, 72-74
NHS Sight Tests and Vouchers for Glasses, 74-75
NHS Vouchers for help with Optical Costs, 75-76
NHS Wig and Fabric Supports, 77

One-Parent Benefit, 21-22
Open Learning, 89
Open University, 129
Optical Costs, Vouchers for help with, 75-76
Orphan's Pension, 122
Over 80s Pension, 134

Pensions, 130-137
Pneumoconiosis, Byssinosis and Miscellaneous
    Diseases Benefits, 67-68
Prescriptions, NHS, 72-74
Prince's Youth Business Trust, The, 97

Restart and Restart Course, 85
Retirement Pension, 130-137

Service Families Working Abroad, 157-158
Severe Disablement Allowance, 59-61
Sickness Benefit, 53-56
Sickness Benefits, Overview, 50
Sight Tests, NHS, 74-75
Social Fund Cold Weather Payments, 48-49
Social Fund Funeral Payments, 47-48
Social Fund Maternity Payments, 47
Social Fund, Overview, 43-44
Social Security Act 1986, 8

Statutory Maternity Pay, 23-25
Statutory Sick Pay, 50-53
Student Grants, 124-127
Student Loans, 127-128

TAPs, 92
Thirteen-week Job Review, 84
Toward 2000, 12
Training for Work, 89
Travel Costs, Hospital, 76
Travel to Interview Scheme, 86
Treatment Allowance, 119

Unemployability Supplement, 117-118
Unemployment Benefit, 80-84
Unemployment Benefits, Overview, 80
Union Law, 111

Vacancies Register, 84
Vaccine Damage Payments, 65-66
Vitamins, Free, 77-78
Vouchers for Glasses, 74-75

War Disablement Pension Awards, 116-117
War Disablement Pension, 115-116
War Pensioners' Welfare Service, 123
War Pensions Agency, 113
War Pensions, Overview, 114
War Widow's Pension, 121-122
War Widower's Pension, 122
Widow's Benefits, Overview, 37
Widow's Payment, 37
Widow's Pension, 38-39
Widowed Mother's Allowance, 38
Wigs, NHS, 77
Work Trial, 86-87

Youth Training, 88